Contents

Chapter 1
What is a Spreadsheet?

Getting Started

A spreadsheet is a very useful piece of computer software mainly used for working with numbers. Spreadsheets are used in thousands of different applications which involve doing calculations or drawing charts.

Spreadsheets are often used for planning budgets and working with financial data. Different figures can be entered and the effect of the changes will be calculated automatically.

Microsoft Excel is one of many different spreadsheet packages. In Excel, spreadsheets are referred to as workbooks. Just to make it even more confusing, a workbook can contain several worksheets.

In this chapter you will learn how to move around a worksheet and enter text and numbers.

 Load Microsoft Excel. You can do this in one of two ways:

 Either double-click the Excel icon on your windows desktop

 Or click Start at the bottom left of the screen, then click Programs, then click

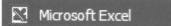

Your screen will look like Figure 1.1:

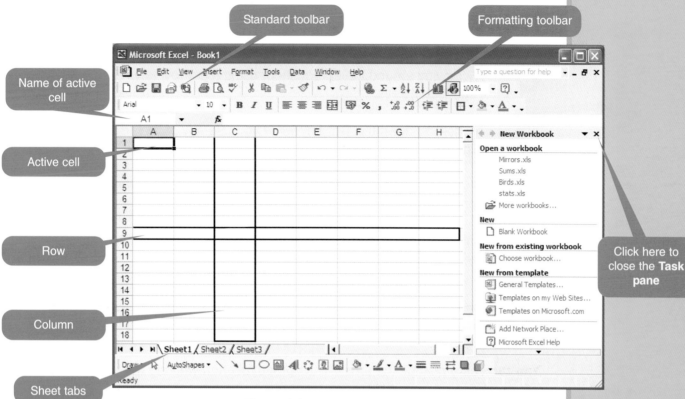

Figure 1.1

A worksheet contains 256 **columns** and 16,384 **rows** – you can only see a few of these on the screen.

The columns are labelled **A**, **B**, **C** and so on. The rows are labelled **1**, **2**, **3** etc.

The worksheet is divided into cells in which you can type a number, a label or a formula. The address of the cell in the top left-hand corner is **A1**, because it is in **column A** and **row 1**.

A **workbook** contains several blank **worksheets** named Sheet1, Sheet2, Sheet3 etc. These names are on the **sheet tabs** shown in Figure 1.1.

Moving around the worksheet

When you open a new workbook, cell **A1** is highlighted, showing that it is the **active cell**. When you start typing, the letters or numbers will appear in this cell.

You can move around the spreadsheet to make a cell active in any of these ways:

Move the pointer using the mouse and click the left mouse button in the cell you want.

Use one of the arrow keys to go up, down, left or right.

Use the **Page Up** or **Page Down** keys.

Press the **Tab** key.

Experiment!

▶ Try moving around the spreadsheet using the arrow keys and Page Up, Page Down keys.

▶ Try holding down the Ctrl key while you use any of the arrow keys. What happens?

▶ What is the name (i.e. address or cell reference) of the very last cell in the worksheet? ~~A1048576~~ xFD1048576

▶ With the active cell somewhere in the middle of the worksheet, try pressing Ctrl-Home. Where does this take you?

The Zoom tool

You can easily change the size of the spreadsheet on your screen.

`100%  ▼`

▶ Make sure you can see the Zoom tool on the Standard toolbar.

▶ Enter a higher percentage to make the sheet bigger, or a smaller percentage to make the sheet smaller and view more of the page on the screen.

Toolbars

You will learn about what individual toolbars and buttons do as they become relevant whilst you are creating your spreadsheet. Below are a few tips that apply to all toolbars, and will be a useful guide if you find that you cannot find a particular toolbar or think that you are missing a button or two! You may find that you already know most of this – it will be pretty much the same as you have experienced in other Microsoft applications such as Word or PowerPoint.

Hiding and displaying toolbars

You can select which toolbars are displayed on your screen. If you find that you can't find a particular button it might be worth checking that you have the right toolbar ticked.

▶ Select View, Toolbars and select the toolbar you want from the list that appears.

Figure 1.2: The Toolbars menu

Customising Toolbars

As well as choosing which toolbars you want displayed, you can also choose which buttons are displayed on each toolbar.

To remove a button from view:

▶ Hold down the **Alt** key, then click and drag the button off the toolbar.

To replace a button:

▶ On the toolbar that the button you want belongs to, click the **Toolbar Options** arrow at the end of the toolbar.

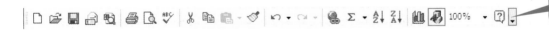

Toolbar Options button

Figure 1.3: The Standard toolbar

▶ Click **Add or Remove Buttons**, then select the name of the toolbar (e.g. **Formatting** or **Standard**), then click to select and deselect buttons.

▶ Click away from the menu when you have finished editing the buttons.

Using the Help functions

If at any time you aren't sure how to do something in **Excel**, you can search the **Help** files for instructions on your chosen subject. For example, let's search for help on **copying and pasting**.

 Select **Help**, **Microsoft Excel Help** from the menu.

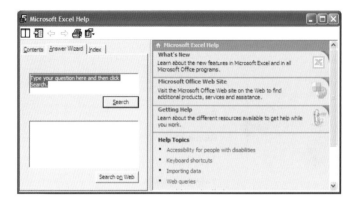

Figure 1.4: The Help Answer Wizard

Notice that there are three tabs titled **Contents**, **Answer Wizard** and **Index**. These are all different ways of finding help on your chosen subject. The easiest one to use is usually the **Answer Wizard**, so make sure that tab is selected.

 Type **copying and pasting** into the **Search** box, then press the **Search** button.

There's a lot of information here! In the bottom left box there is a list of different copying and pasting topics. The right-hand pane displays more detail on whichever topic is highlighted in the bottom left box.

 Display more detail on how to **Move or copy cells** by clicking that subject in the bottom left box.

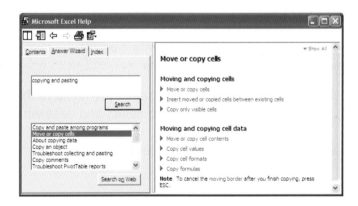

Figure 1.5

The right-hand pane should now talk you through how to move or copy cells.

  Click the **Close** icon to close the **Help** window.

6

Entering data

Suppose that you have to produce a list of all the employees in an office along with the number of days holiday they have taken so far this year.

The list will look like this:

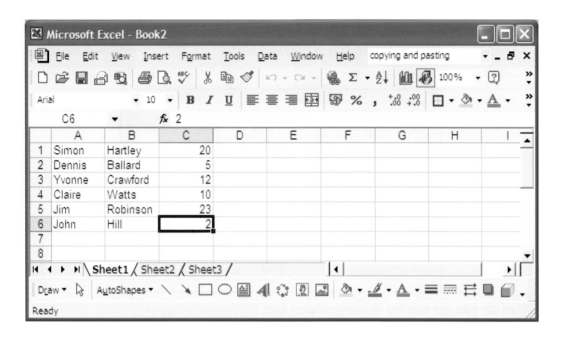

Figure 1.6

Tip:
If you start to type another name beginning with, say S in cell **A7**, Excel will guess that you are going to type **Simon** again and enter the letters for you. If you were going to type **Simon**, you can just tab out of the cell or press **Enter**. If you were going to type **Stuart** or some other name beginning with **S**, just carry on typing. Try it out.

▶ Click in cell **A1**.

▶ Type the name **Simon**.

▶ Press the right arrow key.

▶ Type the surname **Hartley**. Press the right arrow key again and type the number **20** in cell **C1**.

▶ Press **Enter**. Excel guesses that you are typing a list and goes to cell **A2**. (If it does not, click in cell **A2** or use the arrow keys to go there).

▶ Copy the rest of the list. If you make any mistakes, don't worry because you can correct them in a minute.

Editing data

One name has been spelt wrongly. It should be spelt Clare, not Claire. There are several ways of putting it right.

First way

▶ Click in the cell containing the name Claire. You will see that the name appears in the formula bar, as shown below.

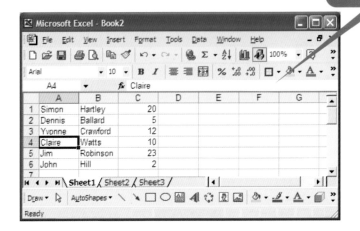

Figure 1.7

Click in the formula bar. Use the arrow keys to move the insertion point between **i** and **r**, and then press the **Backspace** key. You will see that the change is made in the cell **A3** at the same time as you edit the name in the formula bar.

▶ Press **Enter** to register the change.

Second way

Another way to edit a cell is simply to type over the text in the cell. Suppose **Simon's** surname is actually **Hemmings**, not **Hartley**.

▶ Click in the cell containing the surname **Hartley**.

▶ Type **Hemmings**.

▶ Press **Enter**.

Deleting the contents of a cell

To delete the contents of a cell, click in the cell and then press the **Delete** key.

▶ Delete the surname **Robinson**.

Inserting and deleting rows and columns

We can delete the whole of Row 5 so that no gap is left between Clare's and John's records.

▶ Right-click the row header for row 5 (see Figure 1.8).

▶ Left-click Delete from the shortcut menu which appears.

The entry for John moves up to Row 5.

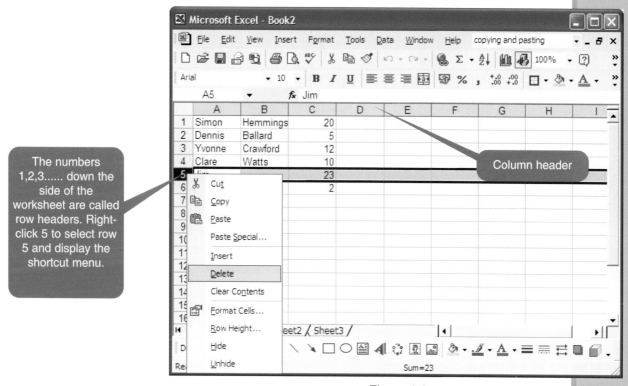

Figure 1.8

Now suppose we want to put a heading at the top of the worksheet, above the names. We need to insert a new row.

▶ Right-click the row header for row 1.

▶ Select Insert from the shortcut menu.

▶ Click the left mouse button in cell A1.

▶ Type Holiday Days Taken in cell A1 in the new row. Press Enter.

▶ Insert another blank line below the header in the same way.

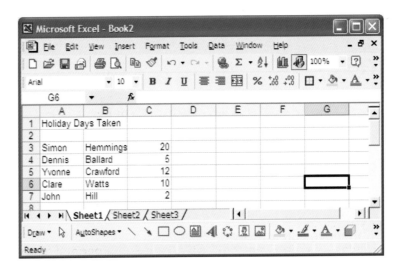

Figure 1.9

Saving your work

▶ Click **File**, **Save** from the main menu.

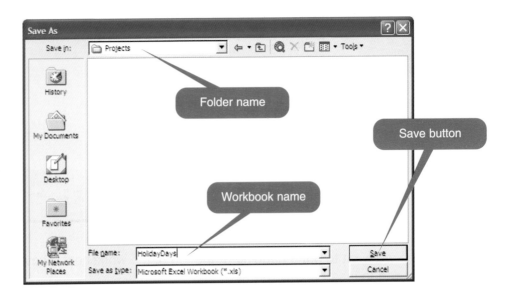

Figure 1.10

Excel gives your workbook the default name **Book1.xls**. The name appears in the **File name** box.

▶ Make sure the right folder is displayed in the **Save in** box, then enter the name **HolidayDays** in the **File name** box.

▶ Click the **Save** button to save the workbook.

▶ Close the workbook by selecting **File**, **Close** from the menu.

▶ Close **Excel** by clicking the close icon in the top right of the window.

Chapter 2
Formulae

The really useful part of spreadsheets is formulae. Using a formula Excel will perform calculations for you automatically.

To see how formulae work in Excel, we'll start by doing a page of 'sums'. We'll be using the following mathematical symbols:

+   add

-     subtract

*   multiply

/   divide

()   brackets are used whenever necessary

The first task is to set out the page just how you want it.

Project: Create a worksheet to do calculations

	A	B	C	D	E	F	G
1	ADD		SUBTRACT		DIVIDE		MULTIPLY
2	100		100		230		57.3
3	400		56		14.5		12.5
4							

Figure 2.1

Open up **Excel**; a new blank workbook should automatically be created.

Type the text **ADD**, **SUBTRACT**, **DIVIDE**, **MULTIPLY** in cells **A1**, **C1**, **E1** and **G1** as shown in Figure 2.1.

Type all the numbers as shown in the correct cells.

Tip:
If a new workbook doesn't appear when you open Excel, just click the **New** button on the Standard toolbar.

Selecting cells

In order to format the text in certain cells by making it bold or changing the font, the cells first have to be **selected**. Try the following ways to select a range of cells:

▶ Click in the intersection of the row and column headers to select every cell in the worksheet. All the selected cells appear highlighted.

Click here to select the whole worksheet

	A
1	ADD
2	100
3	100

▶ Click in column header **A** to select column **A**. The new selection replaces the previous one.

▶ Click in row header **1** to select row **1**.

▶ Drag the mouse across cells **A1** to **G1** to select those cells.

▶ To select just cells **A1**, **C1**, **E1** and **G1**, click in cell **A1** and then hold down the **Ctrl** key while you click each of the other cells.

Making text bold

You can format text in a worksheet in a very similar way to **Microsoft Word**.

▶ Make sure cells **A1** to **G1** are selected.

B ▶ Press the **Bold** button on the **Formatting** toolbar.

Inserting a border

Cells **A4**, **C4**, **E4** and **G4** need a thick top and bottom border.

▶ Click In cell **A4**. Hold down **Ctrl** while you click each of the other cells to select them.

▶ From the main menu select **Format, Cells…**

▶ A dialogue box should appear. Click the **Border** tab.

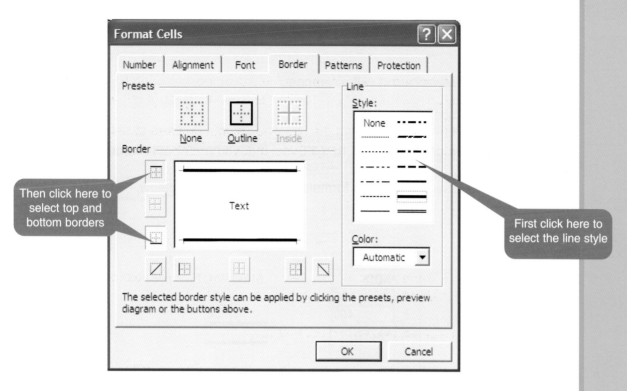

Figure 2.2: The Format Cells dialogue box

▶ Select the line style by clicking a thick line in the **Style** box.

▶ Click the **Border** boxes as shown above to specify top and bottom boxes.

▶ Click **OK**.

▶ Click away from the cells and you will see that all the cells you selected now have a top and bottom border.

	A	B	C	D	E	F	G	H
1	ADD		SUBTRACT		DIVIDE		MULTIPLY	
2	100		100		230		57.3	
3	400		56		14.5		12.5	
4								
5								

Figure 2.3

▶ Before you do any more work, save the workbook, naming it **Sums**.

Tip:
You don't need to click **File, Save** - you can just click the **Save** icon.

Entering formulae

Formulae are entered using cell references.

▶ Click in cell **A4**.

▶ Type an equals sign (=) to tell Excel that you are about to enter a formula.

▶ Type **a2+a3** so that the formula appears as shown below.

	A	B	C	D
	IF	▼ ✗ ✓ *fx* =a2+a3		
1	ADD		SUBTRACT	
2	100		100	
3	400		56	
4	=a2+a3			
5				

Figure 2.4

▶ Press **Enter**. The answer appears!

▶ In cell **C4**, type =c2-c3 and press **Enter**.

▶ In cell **E4**, type =e2/e3 and press **Enter**.

▶ In cell **G4**, type =g2*g3 and press **Enter**.

Tip:
Don't forget to type the equals (=) sign!

Now your worksheet should look like this:

	A	B	C	D	E	F	G	H
1	ADD		SUBTRACT		DIVIDE		MULTIPLY	
2	100		100		230		57.3	
3	400		56		14.5		12.5	
4	500		44		15.86207		716.25	
5								

Figure 2.5

Automatic recalculation

The great thing about a spreadsheet is that once you have entered the formula, you can change the contents of the other cells and the answers will still be right.

▶ Change cell **A2** to **75**. What is the answer now?

▶ Delete the contents of cells **C2** and **C3** by selecting them and then pressing the **Delete** key. What is the answer in cell **C4**?

Standard error values

If you try and make Excel do a formula it can't, an error value will appear instead of an answer.

For example, let's try and divide a number by zero:

▶ Replace the contents of the cell **E3** with **0** and click **Enter**. Now Excel will try and divide **230** by **0** – the answer when you divide anything by zero is **infinity**, which isn't a number. What answer does Excel give?

	A	B	C	D	E	F	G	H
1	ADD		SUBTRACT		DIVIDE		MULTIPLY	
2	75				230		57.3	
3	400				0		12.5	
4	475		0		#DIV/0!		716.25	

Figure 2.6

ℹ Whenever Excel returns **#DIV/0!** as the answer to a formula, it is because it is trying to divide something by zero.

▶ Delete the contents of cell **G2** by selecting it and pressing the **Delete** key. Enter a space in the cell by pressing the **Space** bar then press **Enter**. The cell is empty, but an error message has appeared in cell **G4**.

ℹ If you ask Excel to do a calculation on a non-numeric value, it will give the error message **#VALUE!**.

	A	B	C	D	E	F	G	H
1	ADD		SUBTRACT		DIVIDE		MULTIPLY	
2	75				230			
3	400				0		12.5	
4	475		0		#DIV/0!		#VALUE!	
5								

Figure 2.7

Entering formulae by pointing

Instead of typing in a formula such as **=a2+a3** you can use the mouse to point to the cells in the formula.

▶ Restore the worksheet to how it looks in Figure 2.5. Delete all the formulae in row **4**.

▶ In cell **A4**, type **=** and then click the mouse in cell **A2**.

▶ Type **+** and then click the mouse in cell **A3**.

▶ Press **Enter**. Try entering the other formulae in the same way.

▶ When you have finished experimenting, save your workbook.

Formatting cells

It is sometimes neater to have a comma to indicate thousands. For example, 1,532,000 is easier to read and grasp than 1532000.

We'll format the cells in this spreadsheet to do this.

▶ Click in cell **A2** and drag across to cell **G3**. Right-click in the selection and select **Format Cells** from the list.

▶ Click the **Number** tab in the **Format Cells** dialogue box. Select **Number** from the left-hand list, and click the check box for **Use 1000 Separator (,)**.

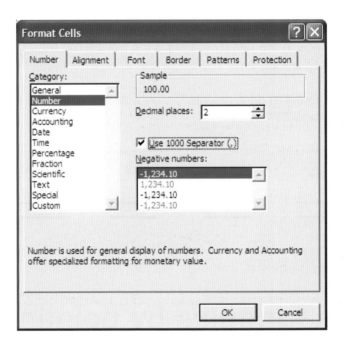

Figure 2.8

▶ Click **OK**. Try entering a value greater than **1000** to see how it is displayed.

▶ Save and close the **Sums** workbook.

Chapter 3
Columns of Data

In this chapter we'll look at changing the way the numbers are displayed in the spreadsheet, and make Excel automatically create column totals.

Project: Create a spreadsheet to hold data on baby statistics

We will create a spreadsheet to hold data about the weights and lengths of newly born babies on a maternity ward.

▶ Open a new Excel workbook.

▶ Type the title **BABY STATISTICS** in cell **A1**. It will overflow the cell, but that's OK. Press **Enter**.

▶ Select cell **A1** again and make it bold by clicking the **Bold** button.

▶ Now add the title **SOMERVILLE WARD** in cell **D1**. Make it **Bold**. —————————— **B**

Changing column widths

You can change the width of column A so the title **Baby Statistics** fits into cell **A1**.

▶ Position the pointer so that it is on the line between column headers **A** and **B**. The pointer will change to a double-headed arrow.

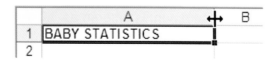

Figure 3.1

▶ Press the left mouse button and hold it down while you drag to the right. The column will widen. Make it wide enough to contain the whole title.

▶ Now type the rest of the column headings as shown in Figure 3.2.

Now try a second way of widening a column.

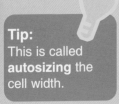
▶ Position the pointer between the column headers of columns **D** and **E** containing the words **Somerville Ward**.

▶ Double-click the left mouse button. The column automatically widens to fit the heading.

▶ Save your workbook, calling it **Stats**.

Formatting numbers

▶ Now fill in the rest of the headings, months and numbers.

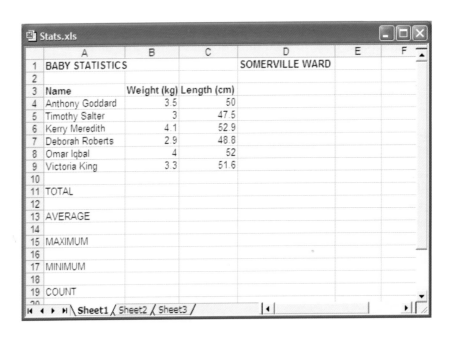

Figure 3.2

Notice that data starting with a letter is automatically **left-justified** in a cell. **Numeric** data on the other hand is automatically **right-justified**.

The measurements would look much better if they were all shown to **2** decimal places. At the moment, if a measurement is entered as **3.0**, Excel automatically shortens this to **3**.

▶ Select cells **B4** to **C19** by dragging across them.

 ▶ Click the **Increase Decimal** button on the **Formatting** toolbar.

All the measurements should now be shown to **2** decimal places, as shown in Figure 3.3.

	A	B	C	D	E	F	G
1	BABY STATISTICS			SOMERVILLE WARD			
2							
3	Name	Weight (kg)	Length (cm)				
4	Anthony Goddard	3.50	50.00				
5	Timothy Salter	3.00	47.50				
6	Kerry Meredith	4.10	52.90				
7	Deborah Roberts	2.90	48.80				
8	Omar Iqbal	4.00	52.00				
9	Victoria King	3.30	51.60				
10							
11	TOTAL						
12							
13	AVERAGE						
14							
15	MAXIMUM						
16							
17	MINIMUM						
18							
19	COUNT						
20							

Figure 3.3

Adding a column of numbers

We want to add up each of the baby's weights to get the total weight of all the babies on the ward.

▶ Click in cell **B11** to make it the active cell.

▶ Click the **AutoSum** button on the **Standard** toolbar. ——————

Excel guesses which cells you want to sum. Your screen will look like the one below.

IF ▾ ✕ ✓ ƒx =SUM(B4 B10)

	A	B	C	D	E
1	BABY STATISTICS			SOMERVILLE WARD	
2					
3	Name	Weight (kg)	Length (cm)		
4	Anthony Goddard	3.50	50.00		
5	Timothy Salter	3.00	47.50		
6	Kerry Meredith	4.10	52.90		
7	Deborah Roberts	2.90	48.80		
8	Omar Iqbal	4.00	52.00		
9	Victoria King	3.30	51.60		
10					
11	TOTAL	=SUM(B4 B10)			
12		SUM(**number1**, [number2], ...)			
13	AVERAGE				
14					
15	MAXIMUM				
16					
17	MINIMUM				
18					
19	COUNT				
20					

Figure 3.4: The AutoSum function

▶ Press **Enter**. The answer appears.

▶ Find the total **Length** of all the babies on the ward.

Tip:
It is a good idea to include cell **B10** in the **Sum** formula. If you later need to add an extra row, you can insert it above **Row 10** and the **Sum** formula will still be correct.

 ▷ Save your workbook.

In the next chapter we'll look at the other functions such as Average, Minimum and Maximum.

Renaming a worksheet

You can change the names of the worksheets to something more meaningful than Sheet1 and Sheet2.

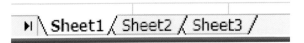

▷ Right-click on the Sheet1 sheet tab.

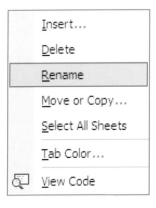

Tip:
You can also rename a sheet by double-clicking the sheet tab then typing a new name.

▷ Select Rename from the shortcut menu that appears. The text on the sheet tab is now selected.

▷ Now type Birth Stats. The text will appear on the sheet tab. Just click away from the sheet tab when you have finished typing.

▷ Repeat this for Sheet2, renaming it Daily Weights.

Inserting and deleting sheets

Tip:
If you try to delete a worksheet that has data in it, you will see a warning message confirming that you want to delete the sheet.

▷ To delete Sheet3, right-click the sheet tab then select Delete from the shortcut menu that appears.

▷ To insert a new sheet between Birth Stats and Daily Weights, right-click the Daily Weights sheet and select Insert from the shortcut menu.

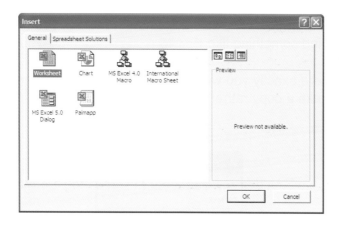

Figure 3.5: Inserting a worksheet

▶ Make sure **Worksheet** is selected then click **OK**.

Figure 3.6

Copying a worksheet

You can copy a worksheet within a spreadsheet or between open spreadsheets.

▶ Open a new workbook by clicking the **New** icon on the **Standard** toolbar.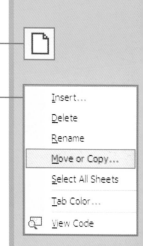

▶ In the **Stats** spreadsheet, right-click the **Birth Stats** worksheet and select **Move or Copy** from the menu.

You are now asked where you want to copy or move it to.

Figure 3.7

○ In the first drop-down list, select the new workbook you have just opened, it will be called something like **Book5**.

○ Select where exactly you want the sheet to be put in the second list box. We want to make a copy rather than move it, so click on the **Create a copy** check box.

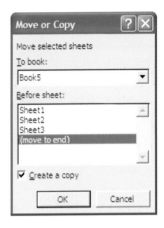

Figure 3.8

○ Click **OK**. The worksheet should now be copied to the new workbook.

ⓘ Note that if you wanted to move a worksheet to another workbook you would use the same method, but without clicking the **Create a copy** check box.

○ You can now close the workbook you have just opened (**Book5**). There is no need to save it.

Moving worksheets

○ You can easily move worksheets by first selecting a sheet, then clicking and dragging it to the new position.

Figure 3.9: Click and drag the sheet tab

Figure 3.10: Drop the sheet tab to the right of Daily Weights

 ○ Save the **Stats** workbook. You will need it again in the next chapter so you don't need to close it.

Chapter 4
Functions

In this chapter you will continue to work on the Stats spreadsheet that you started in the last chapter. You'll learn how to use some of Excel's built-in functions to calculate the average, maximum and minimum baby weights and lengths.

A function is a formula used in a calculation. Excel provides over 200 functions to help with business, scientific and engineering applications. Don't worry, you only need 3 or 4 at this stage!

  Load the spreadsheet Stats that you created in the last chapter, if it is not already open.

It should look something like the one below. The Formula bar and the active cell have been labelled in the screenshot.

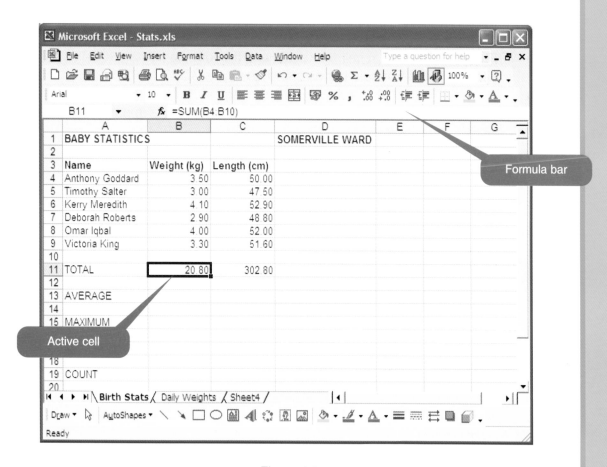

Figure 4.1

The SUM function

You have already used one of Excel's built-in functions – the **SUM** function.

Look at the **Formula bar** in the screenshot above. It tells you what formula has been used to get the answer **20.80** in the active cell, **B11**.

You entered the **SUM** function by pressing the **AutoSum** button. Adding up a row or column of numbers is such a common task in spreadsheet work that this special shortcut button is provided.

You can also enter a function by typing it into the cell. We'll try that now.

- ▶ Click in cell **B11**.

- ▶ Press the **Delete** key to delete the formula currently in the cell.

- ▶ Type **=sum(** in the cell (including the open bracket).

- ▶ Now click in cell **B4** and hold the left mouse button down while you drag down to cell **B10**. Notice that Excel is automatically filling in the formula as you do this in both the cell and the Formula bar.

- ▶ Type **)** to finish the formula.

- ▶ Press **Enter**. Click in cell **B11** again and the formula **=SUM(B4:B10)** appears in the Formula bar as shown in Figure 4.1.

You'll find out why we included the blank cell **B10** in the formula in a minute.

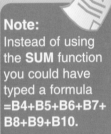

Note:
Instead of using the **SUM** function you could have typed a formula **=B4+B5+B6+B7+ B8+B9+B10**.

The AVERAGE function

The **AVERAGE** function works in much the same way as the **SUM** function.

- ▶ Click in cell **B13**.

- ▶ Type **=average(**.

- ▶ Click in cell **B4** and drag down to cell **B10**. Type **)** to finish the formula.

- ▶ Press **Enter**. The answer, **3.47**, appears in the cell.

- ▶ In cell **C13** find the average length of all the babies (it should be **50.47**).

Tip:
You can use either upper or lower case letters for the function name, or even a mixture of both.

MAX and MIN functions

To find the maximum measurements, you need the MAX function.

▶ Click in cell B15.

▶ Type =max(in the cell (including the opening bracket).

▶ Click in cell B4 and drag down to cell B10. Type) to finish the formula.

▶ Press Enter. The answer, 4.10, appears in the cell.

▶ Now do the same for the maximum length.

▶ Use the MIN function to find the minimums.

Your spreadsheet will look like this:

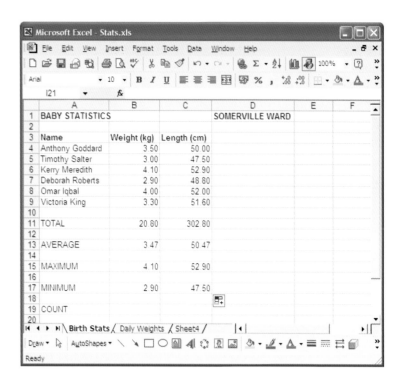

Figure 4.2

The COUNT function

To count the number of babies, you need the COUNT function.

▶ Click in cell B19.

▶ Type =count(. Click in cell B4 then drag down to cell B10. Press Enter.

Excel automatically adds the closing bracket for you. The answer **6.00** should appear in the cell. Notice that although we included **7** rows in the **COUNT** formula, Excel has only counted those rows where a value has been added.

▶ Repeat this for the **Length** column.

▶ Highlight cells **B19** and **C19** then click the **Decrease Decimal** button twice. You can only have whole numbers of babies so we don't need any decimal points!

Adding another record

Suppose another baby is born on the ward and its measurements have to be recorded on the spreadsheet.

▶ Right-click the row header for row **10**. The shortcut menu will appear.

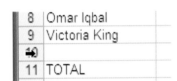

▶ Select **Insert** from the menu to insert a new row.

▶ In the new row, enter the data for **Jacob Walton**, who weighs **3.7kg** and is **51cm** long.

▶ Click in cell **B12** and look at the formula in the formula bar. The formula has automatically adjusted to include the new row – which saves us having to change it!

▶ Now we'll double-underline the title **Baby Statistics**. Select cell **A1** then click in the selection with the right mouse button.

▶ Select **Format Cells** from the shortcut menu.

▶ Click the **Font** tab. Now choose **Double** from the list in the **Underline** box.

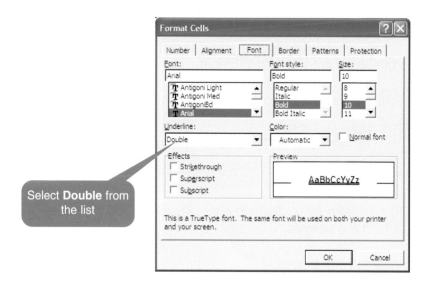

Figure 4.3: The Format Cells dialogue box

 Click **OK**. The spreadsheet will now look like this:

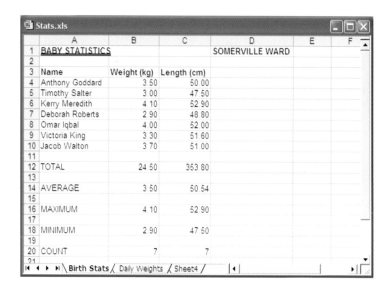

Figure 4.4

If your spreadsheet looks different from this – check the formulae.

If you had not included Row 10 in your formulae originally, the formulae would not have adjusted when you entered a new row. That's because the new row would be outside the range specified in the formulae.

 Save your spreadsheet.

Copying data between sheets

On another sheet in the workbook we are going to create a chart to record the weights of all the babies over the first 5 days. We can copy the titles and names of all the babies to save us typing them in again.

▶ Make sure the **Birth Stats** sheet is selected. Select cells **A1** to **D1**.

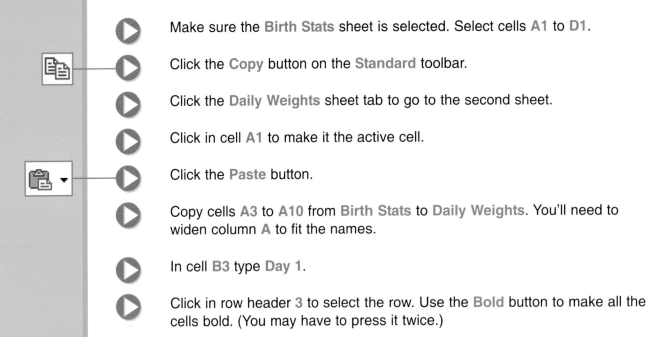

▶ Click the **Copy** button on the **Standard** toolbar.

▶ Click the **Daily Weights** sheet tab to go to the second sheet.

▶ Click in cell **A1** to make it the active cell.

▶ Click the **Paste** button.

▶ Copy cells **A3** to **A10** from **Birth Stats** to **Daily Weights**. You'll need to widen column **A** to fit the names.

▶ In cell **B3** type **Day 1**.

▶ Click in row header **3** to select the row. Use the **Bold** button to make all the cells bold. (You may have to press it twice.)

Now your worksheet should look similar to the one below.

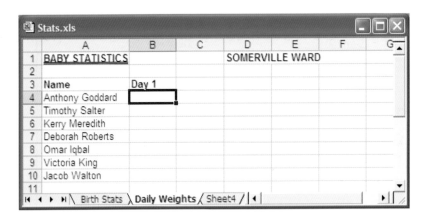

Figure 4.5

Filling a series

Instead of typing all the other days, Day 2, Day 3 etc in cells **C3** to **F3**, you can let Excel do it for you.

▶ Click cell **B3**.

▶ Click and drag the small black handle in the bottom right hand corner of the cell. This is called the **Fill handle**. Drag it to cell **F3**.

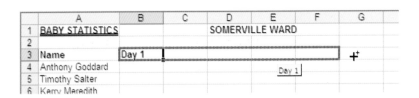

Figure 4.6: Filling a series

Now your headings should look like this:

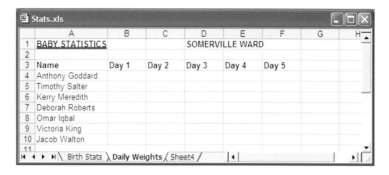

Figure 4.7

 Save your workbook.

Hide or unhide rows and columns

Hiding rows and columns is useful if you don't want certain data to appear on a printout, or simply to make data in a large spreadsheet easier to view on screen.

Hiding rows

We'll hide the **Total** row (**Row 12**) in the **Stats** spreadsheet.

 Click on the **Birth Stats** tab to make it the active sheet.

 Click anywhere in **Row 12**.

 Select **Format**, **Row**, **Hide** from the menu.

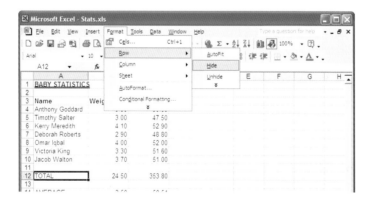

Figure 4.8: Hiding a row

Row 12 is now hidden – notice that there is no Row 12 row header.

Unhiding rows

 Select two cells in rows **11** and **13** (see figure 4.9).

9	Victoria King		3.30		51.(
10	Jacob Walton		3.70		51.(
11					
13					
14	AVERAGE		3.50		50.!
15					

Figure 4.9

▶ Select **Format**, **Row**, **Unhide** from the menu.

Row 12 should now be visible.

Hiding and unhiding columns

▶ Hide **Column C** by clicking anywhere in it, then selecting **Format**, **Column**, **Hide** from the menu.

▶ Unhide **Column C** by selecting cells in columns **B** and **D**, then selecting **Format**, **Column**, **Unhide** from the menu.

Freeze row and column titles

In a big spreadsheet, it is useful to have the row and column titles frozen so that no matter where you scroll in the spreadsheet you can see them.

First we'll make the **Stats** spreadsheet a bit bigger.

▶ Make **Daily Weights** the active sheet.

▶ In cell **F3**. Use the **Fill Handle** to extend the headings to **Day 50**.

▶ Click in cell **A11** and type **Baby 1**. Use the fill handle to enter babies **2** to **50**.

▶ To freeze the row and column titles, you have to place the cursor in **the nearest cell to A1 that you don't want frozen**. That sounds like a bit of a mouthful! Basically, we need **Column A** frozen, and **Row 3** frozen. For this we need to make cell **B4** the active cell.

▶ Select **Window**, **Freeze Panes** from the menu.

Black lines will appear next to the frozen panes.

	A	B	C	D	E	F	G	H
1	BABY STATISTICS			SOMERVILLE WARD				
2								
3	Name	Day 1	Day 2	Day 3	Day 4	Day 5	Day 6	Day 7
4	Anthony Goddard							
5	Timothy Salter							
6	Kerry Meredith							
7	Deborah Roberts							
8	Omar Iqbal							
9	Victoria King							
10	Jacob Walton							
11	Baby 1							
12	Baby 2							
13	Baby 3							

Figure 4.10: Freezing panes

▶ Scroll across to Day 50 – the baby names should still be visible. This would be invaluable for anyone entering data, else they would have to scroll left to see which baby was in each row before entering the data.

▶ Now try scrolling down to Baby 50 to see the effect of the frozen column headings.

Unfreezing panes

▶ Select Window, Unfreeze Panes from the menu. It doesn't matter which cell is the active cell for this.

The black lines will disappear.

Opening several workbooks

This is very straightforward. You can open a second spreadsheet in just the same way you did the first.

With the Stats spreadsheet open, either

▶ Click the New icon on the Standard toolbar to open a new spreadsheet, *or*

▶ Click Open on the Standard toolbar to open a previously created spreadsheet.

ⓘ To flick between workbooks, *either* select Window from the menu then the sheet you want *or*

ⓘ Use the buttons at the bottom of your screen.

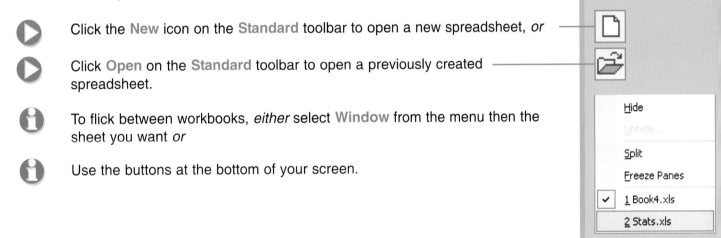

Saving under another name

ⓘ To save an existing workbook under a different name, open the workbook then select File, Save As from the menu. You will then be asked where you want to save it and what name you want to save it under.

Saving as a different file type

By default, Excel will save your workbooks as **.xls** files, but you can choose from many other file types.

▶ To save a file as a different file type, select **File**, **Save As** from the menu.

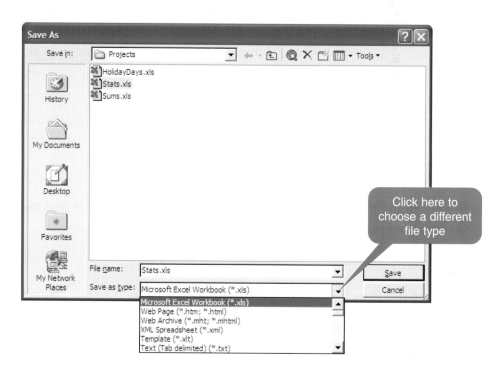

Figure 4.11: Saving as a different file type

▶ Type a name for the file in the **File name** box, and choose a folder location for the file.

▶ Click the down arrow in the **Save as type** box to view all the different file types. Select the one you want, then click **Save**.

▶ Close the **Stats** workbook.

Chapter 5
Charts

Charts are a very good way of presenting information so that it is easy to grasp immediately.

In this chapter we'll look at how the number of songbirds in the UK has declined over the past 3 decades.

This alarming decline is partly due to modern farming methods. Many hedgerows, meadows and marshes have disappeared, so birds have nowhere to live. Chemicals sprayed on fields kill insects that birds need for food.

Project: Draw charts relating to the number of songbirds in England

Decline in songbird numbers between 1972 and 1996

(Numbers given in millions)

	1972	1996
Skylark	7.72	3.09
Willow warbler	6.06	4.67
Linnet	1.56	0.925
Song thrush	3.62	1.74
Lapwing	0.588	0.341
Yellowhammer	4.4	1.76
Blackbird	12.54	8.4
Tree sparrow	0.65	0.0845
Corn bunting	0.144	0.03

Source: British Trust for Ornithology

Figure 5.1

 Open a new workbook. ———————————————

Type the headings and the names of the birds in the survey as shown below.

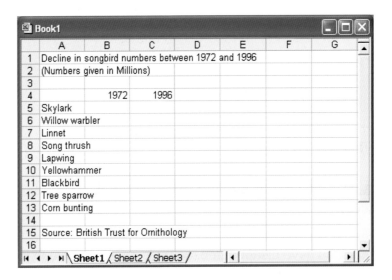

Figure 5.2

Position the pointer between the column headers **A** and **B**. Drag to the right to widen column **A**.

Click in row header **1**, and hold down the **Ctrl** key while you click in row headers **4** and **15**. This selects all three rows.

Click the **Bold** button on the **Formatting** toolbar to make these rows bold.

Click in cell **A15** and press the **Italic** button to make it italic.

Enter the data given on the previous page.

When you have done that, your spreadsheet will look like this:

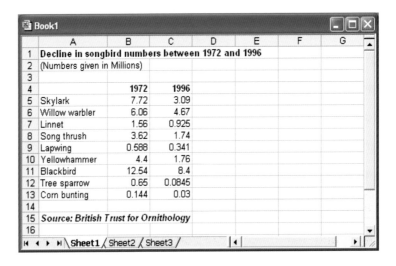

Figure 5.3

Save your workbook, naming it **Birds**.

Sorting data

It would be neater if the birds were sorted in alphabetical order.

▶ First we need to select the data we want to sort. Click to select cell **A5** and drag to cell **C13**.

▶ Select **Data**, **Sort** from the menu.

▶ We want to sort by the bird names, which is **Column A**. Fill in the boxes as shown below.

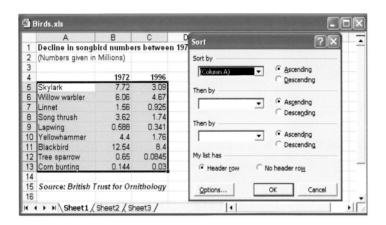

Figure 5.4: The Sort dialogue box

▶ Click **OK**. The names should now be sorted.

	A	B	C	D	E	F
1	Decline in songbird numbers between 1972 and 1996					
2	(Numbers given in Millions)					
3						
4		1972	1996			
5	Blackbird	12.54	8.4			
6	Corn bunting	0.144	0.03			
7	Lapwing	0.588	0.341			
8	Linnet	1.56	0.925			
9	Skylark	7.72	3.09			
10	Song thrush	3.62	1.74			
11	Tree sparrow	0.65	0.0845			
12	Willow warbler	6.06	4.67			
13	Yellowhammer	4.4	1.76			
14						
15	Source: British Trust for Ornithology					
16						

Figure 5.5

Drawing a bar chart

Now we can draw a bar chart to show this data.

▶ Click in **A4** and drag diagonally through to **C13** to select the cells to be charted.

▶ Click the **Chart Wizard** button on the **Standard** toolbar. ————————

You will see a dialogue box like the one in Figure 5.6.

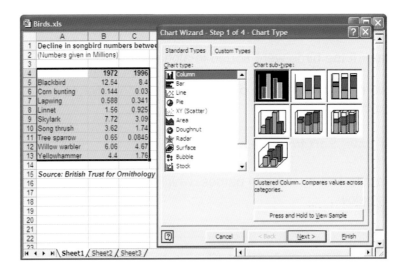

Figure 5.6: The Chart Wizard Step 1

Leave the first **Chart sub-type** selected.

Click and hold **Press and Hold to View Sample** to see what your chart will look like.

You could click **Finish** now for a quick chart, but we will go through steps 2, 3 and 4 to add a title to the chart. Click **Next**.

We don't need to do anything in **Step 2**, so click **Next** again.

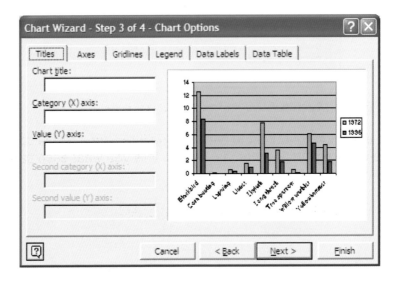

Figure 5.7: The Chart Wizard Step 3

In the **Chart title** box, type **Decline in songbirds 1972-1996** and then click **Next**.

In the **Step 4** dialogue box you can specify where you want the chart to appear. It can either be placed on its own in a new chart sheet, or it can be placed in the current sheet, **Sheet1**.

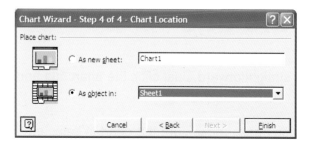

Figure 5.8: The Chart Wizard Step 4

▶ Leave the default, **As Object in Sheet1**. Click **Finish**.

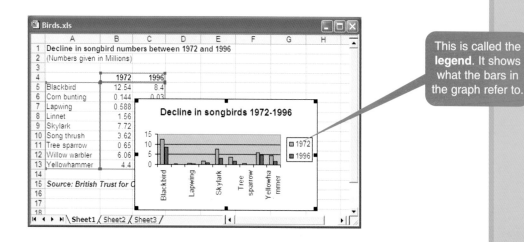

This is called the **legend**. It shows what the bars in the graph refer to.

Figure 5.9

Moving and sizing a chart

You can move the chart so that it does not overlap the data.

▶ Move the pointer around the chart, letting it rest for a few seconds in different places. Notice that the **tool tip** tells you what each part of the chart is called.

▶ See if you can identify parts of the chart called **chart area**, **plot area**, **category axis**, **value axis**, **series "1972"**, **series "1996"**.

▶ Click in the **chart area** and drag the chart below the data.

▶ Drag the bottom right-hand corner handle of the chart to make it bigger. To make it bigger without distorting the shape of the graph, try pressing the **Shift** key whilst dragging the handle.

▶ Click on one of the axes. Edit the font size using the **Font Size** option on the **Formatting** menu at the top of the screen; make sure all the category names appear on the axis.

Tip:
If you right-click the chart title, legend or either axis, a shortcut menu will appear. Using the **Format** option you can change options such as the **Font**.

Deleting the title

▶ This is very straightforward. Just click the chart title and press the **Delete** key.

▶ To add the title again, make sure the chart is selected (it should have small black handles around it) then select **Chart**, **Chart Options** from the main menu.

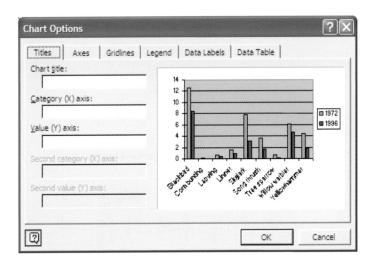

Figure 5.10: The Chart Options dialogue box

The chart options window appears. Notice that you can make changes to many parts of the chart using this window.

▶ Make sure the **Title** tab is selected, then enter the same title as before, **Decline in songbirds 1972-1996**.

▶ Click **OK**.

Adding axis titles

It would be nice to have a data label on the **Y** axis, to make it clear that the figures are in Millions.

▶ Open the **Chart Options** window by selecting **Chart**, **Chart Options** from the menu.

▶ Under the **Title** tab, enter **Millions** in the **Value (Y) axis:** box.

▶ Click **OK**.

ⓘ You can delete the axis title by clicking it to select it, then pressing the **Delete** key.

Changing the background colour

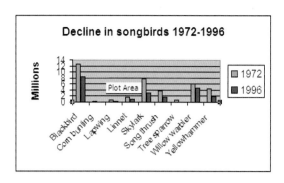

Figure 5.11

▶ Place the cursor over the **Plot Area**. If you're not sure which is the **Plot Area**, just leave the mouse pointer there for a few seconds and the **tool tip** should tell you.

▶ Click the right mouse button. A shortcut menu appears.

▶ Select **Format Plot Area** from the menu.

Here you can change both the border style and colour, and the background colour (the background is the part that is currently grey).

▶ Have a play with the settings, and try a different background colour. Click **OK**.

Tip:
You can always click **Undo** if you don't like the changes!

Changing the colour of the bars

You have to change the colour of the 1972 series separately from the 1996 series. We'll start by changing the 1972 series.

▶ Place the mouse over any bar in the 1972 series. After a few seconds the tool tip should say **Series "1972"** followed by the bird name and number of the particular bar you are on.

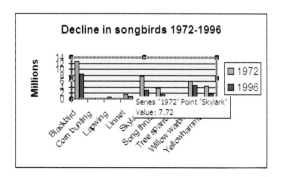

Figure 5.12

▶ Click the right mouse button. The shortcut menu appears.

▶ Click **Format Data Series** on the menu.

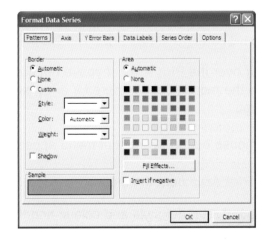

Figure 5.13: The Format Data Series dialogue box

The **Format Data Series** window appears. Here you can change the border around each bar and the fill colour of the bars.

▶ Choose a new fill colour by clicking a colour in the right-hand box, under **Area**. Click **OK**.

▶ Now repeat this for the 1996 series. Follow exactly the same method, but just make sure that you right-click on the 1996 series to start.

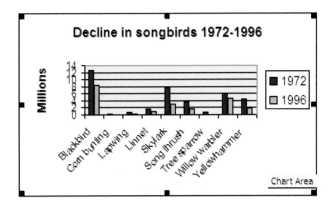

Figure 5.14

 ▶ When you are happy with the way the chart looks, save your spreadsheet.

Chapter 6
Pie Charts

Creating a pie chart

We'll use another sheet in the same workbook to enter some data from the RSPB 2003 Garden Bird Watch Survey (www.rspb.org.uk/birdwatch). We will then use this data to create a pie chart.

▶ Make sure the **Birds** workbook is open.

▶ Click on the tab for Sheet2.

▶ Enter the following data.

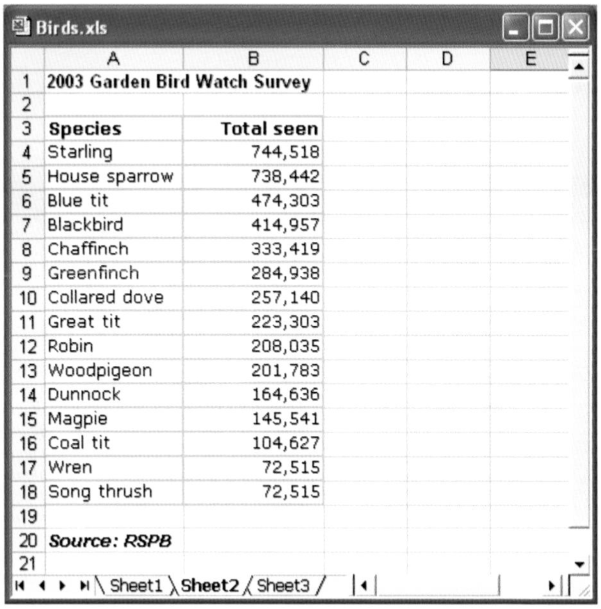

	A	B	C	D	E
1	2003 Garden Bird Watch Survey				
2					
3	**Species**	**Total seen**			
4	Starling	744,518			
5	House sparrow	738,442			
6	Blue tit	474,303			
7	Blackbird	414,957			
8	Chaffinch	333,419			
9	Greenfinch	284,938			
10	Collared dove	257,140			
11	Great tit	223,303			
12	Robin	208,035			
13	Woodpigeon	201,783			
14	Dunnock	164,636			
15	Magpie	145,541			
16	Coal tit	104,627			
17	Wren	72,515			
18	Song thrush	72,515			
19					
20	*Source: RSPB*				
21					

Figure 6.1

▶ Drag across cells **A4** to **B18** to select them.

▶ Click the **Chart Wizard** button on the **Standard** toolbar.

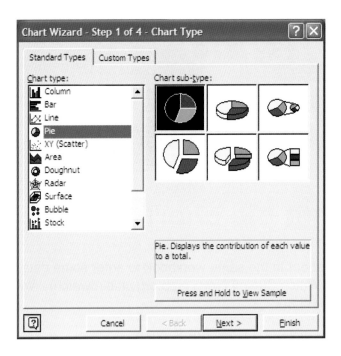

Figure 6.2: The Chart Wizard Step 1

▶ In the dialogue box, select **Pie** from the **Chart type** list box. Leave the first option selected for the **Chart sub-type**. Click **Next**.

▶ Click **Next** in the **Step 2** dialogue box.

▶ Make sure the **Titles** tab is selected. Type the title **Garden Birds 2003**.

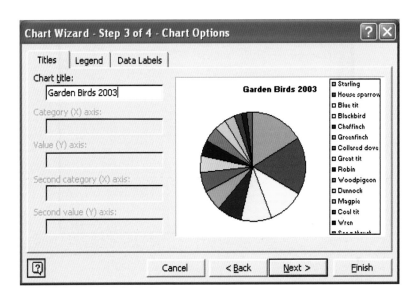

Figure 6.3: The Chart Wizard Step 3

▶ Click the **Legend** tab just to see what the options are.

▶ You can experiment to see where you want to put the legend. In the screenshot below, **Right** has been selected.

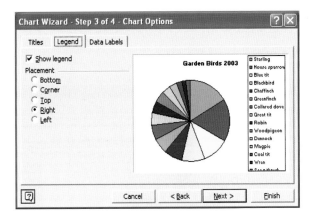

Figure 6.4

▶ Click the **Data Labels** tab.

At the moment **Data Labels** is set to **None**.

▶ Click **Percentage** and **Category Name**.

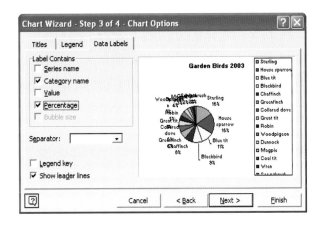

Figure 6.5

▶ Click **Next**.

▶ This time we will place the chart in a separate Chart sheet. Click **As new sheet**.

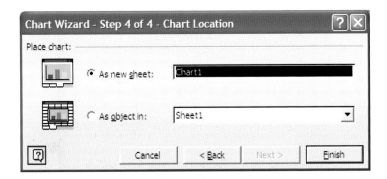

Figure 6.6: The Chart Wizard Step 4

Note:
Don't worry if the labels are muddled – we'll fix this later.

▶ Click **Finish**.

The chart appears in a new **Chart Sheet**.

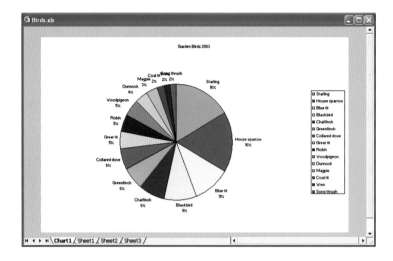

Figure 6.7

Formatting the data labels

We need to make the labels a bit bigger – they're too small to read!

▶ Right-click any of the data labels.

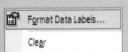

▶ A shortcut menu appears. Click **Format Data Labels**.

The **Format Data Labels** dialogue box appears.

▶ Click the **Font** tab in the dialogue box.

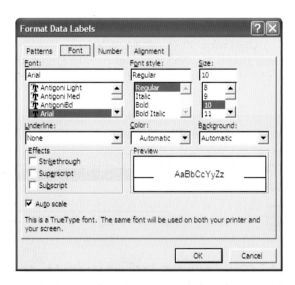

Figure 6.8

▶ Change the font size to **12**. Click **OK**.

▶ If any labels are overlapping, click them and drag them away from each other.

▶ Format the legend so the text is **12** point.

▶ Format the **Chart Title** to **18** point.

▶ Change the title to **Garden Bird Numbers 2003**.

Tip:
To change the text of the **Chart Title,** click it to select it and then click in the text where you want to insert or delete text.

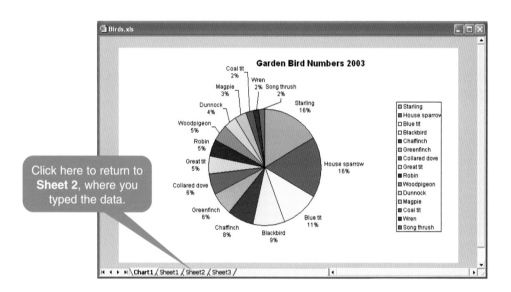

Figure 6.9

▶ Save your workbook.

Copying and pasting charts

We'll copy and paste the pie chart onto a new sheet.

▶ Click once on the **Chart Area** of the pie chart (this is the white background) to select it.

▶ Select **Edit**, **Copy** from the menu.

▶ Click **Sheet3** at the bottom of the screen to select it. Now select **Edit**, **Paste** from the menu.

The pie chart is pasted into **Sheet3**. It's much bigger than we want it so now we'll resize it.

▶ Scroll down so that you can see the bottom right-hand corner of the chart. There should be a small black handle in the corner. If there isn't, try clicking the chart to select it.

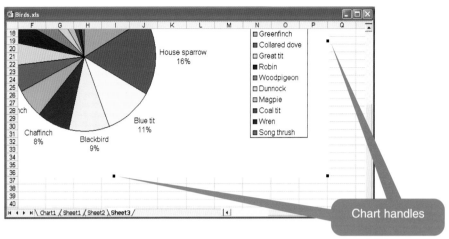

Figure 6.10

 Click and drag the handle towards the top left corner whilst holding down the Shift key, until the chart is a similar size to the one below.

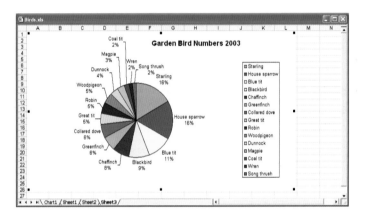

Figure 6.11

Tip:
Holding down the **Shift** key means that the chart will resize in proportion to its original shape.

Changing the chart type

It's easy to change the chart type, for example from a pie chart to a bar or line chart even after you have created it.

 Make sure Sheet3 is selected. Right-click on the Chart Area. The shortcut menu appears.

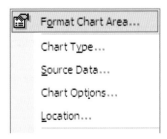

 Select Chart Type from the menu.

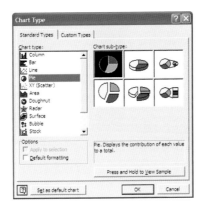

Figure 6.12: The Chart Type dialogue box

Here all you need to do is choose another chart type. Try a **Line** chart. Click **OK**.

It doesn't actually make any sense to make this chart a line chart. Line charts should only be used when the order of the categories along the x-axis has a meaning. In this example, the birds are placed on the x-axis in a random way.

Change the chart type to a column chart.

Delete the labels above each column by right-clicking on a column and selecting **Format Data Series** from the shortcut menu. Refer to the section above where you inserted the labels into the pie chart if you need to.

Tip:
A quicker way of deleting the labels is simply to click on them and press the **Delete** key.

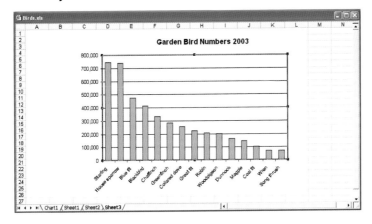

Figure 6.13

Deleting a chart

Now delete the bar chart on **Sheet3** by clicking it to select it, then pressing the **Delete** key.

Save your workbook.

Chapter 7
Printing

Now we're going to try printing various parts from the Birds workbook.

▶ Make sure the Birds workbook is open.

▶ Click Sheet1 to select it.

Figure 7.1

Printing a chart

Firstly we'll see what the chart would look like printed on its own.

▶ Make sure the chart is selected. (It will have handles around it. Click the Chart Area to select it if it is not already selected).

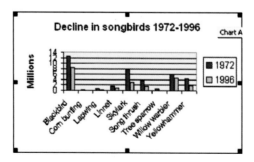

Figure 7.2

Printing the title row on every page

If you have a very large worksheet that spans two or three pages, it is useful to have the title repeated on pages two and three. You can do this in the Page Setup dialogue box.

▶ First we'll set the print area to run onto more than one page. Select cell A1 and drag down to cell K80 or so.

▶ Select File, Print Area, Set Print Area. Click anywhere in the sheet to deselect all the cells.

▶ Go to Print Preview. The document is now 4 pages – 2 pages wide and 2 down. Close Print Preview.

▶ Go to Page Setup by selecting File, Page Setup from the menu.

Tip:
For some reason, if you enter the **Page Setup** dialogue box from **Print Preview**, the option to repeat the title row is deactivated. Make sure you enter **Page Setup** from the **File** menu instead.

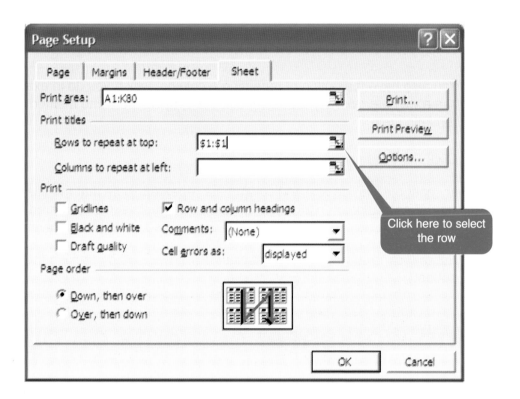

Click here to select the row

Figure 7.9

Here you can either:

▶ type $1:$1 to say row 1

▶ or you can select the cells by clicking the icon on the right of the box. The cursor will become a small horizontal arrow, with which you should point and click row 1.

53

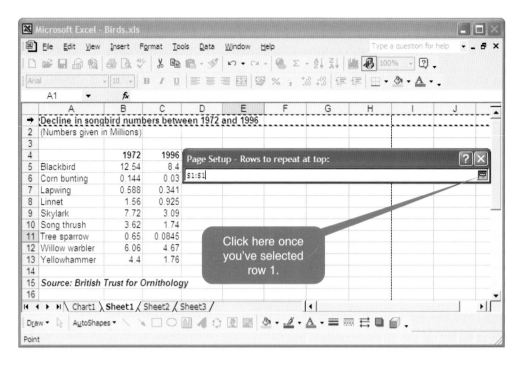

Figure 7.10

- ▶ When you have selected row 1, click the small icon in the right of the box.

- ▶ You also have the option of repeating a column, which you do in exactly the same way as rows. Try repeating column 1, using the same method as for repeating row 1.

- ▶ Click **Print Preview**.

It's not very neat but the title row and column are repeated. Note that the title row and column will only appear on 2 of the 4 sheets. If we'd chosen a print area that was 4 pages long but only one page wide, the title row would appear on every sheet.

- ▶ Either click **Print** and **OK**, or just close **Print Preview** by clicking the **Close** button.

Fitting worksheet contents on one page

Although we've selected a print area that is larger than it needs to be, you are likely to come across spreadsheets that have enough data to fill more than one page. In this case, it is sometimes convenient to try and fit all the data onto one page for printing purposes.

- ▶ Go to **File**, **Page Setup**.

- ▶ Click the **Page** tab.

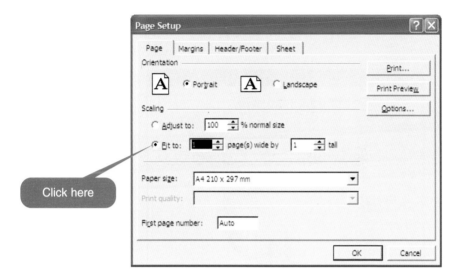

Figure 7.11

▶ Notice the option **Fit to:** under the **Scaling** section. Click the radio button on the left, and leave the other options as **1 page wide by 1 page tall**.

▶ Click **Print Preview**.

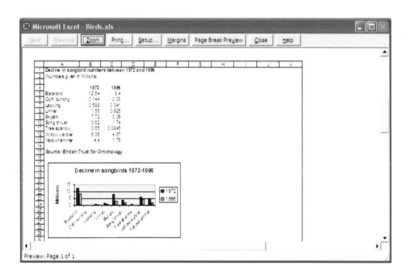

Figure 7.12

The cell range is the same as before, but now there is only 1 page, instead of 4.

▶ Click **Close** to close Print Preview.

Other Page Setup options

Hiding/Unhiding gridlines on printouts

Excel automatically prints without gridlines, but sometimes they can be useful.

▶ Click **Sheet1** to select it. Select **File**, **Page Setup** from the menu.

Click the **Sheet** tab at the top of the **Page Setup** dialogue box.

Tip:
You can also open the **Page Setup** dialogue box by clicking the **Setup** button when you're in **Print Preview.**

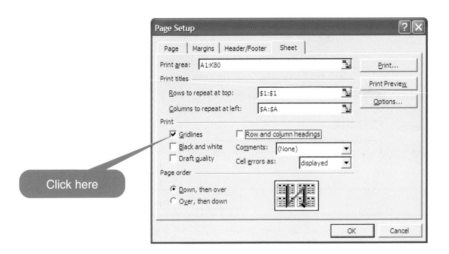

Click here

Figure 7.13

Under the **Print** section, notice there is a check box next to **Gridlines**. Click this to print gridlines.

Now go to **Print Preview** to see what it will look like.

Paper Orientation

In the **Page Setup** dialogue box, click the **Page** tab.

Click the buttons to change the orientation from **Portrait** to **Landscape**.

Paper Size

To change the paper size, click the down-arrow on the right of the box and select the correct paper size.

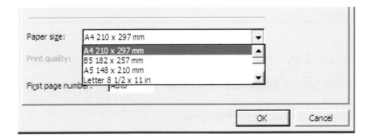

Figure 7.14

Changing the margins

This is also done in **Page Setup**. Just click the **Margins** tab and choose which margin sizes you want.

Click **OK** to close the Page Setup dialogue box.

Chapter 8
Cell Referencing

There are two different ways of referencing a particular cell in a formula.

Relative cell referencing

This is the default setting in Excel. If we take the example in the screenshot below, Excel actually remembers the formula as **=the cell 3 above and one to the left**. This means that when you copy the formula to a different cell, the formula will no longer say **=A1**.

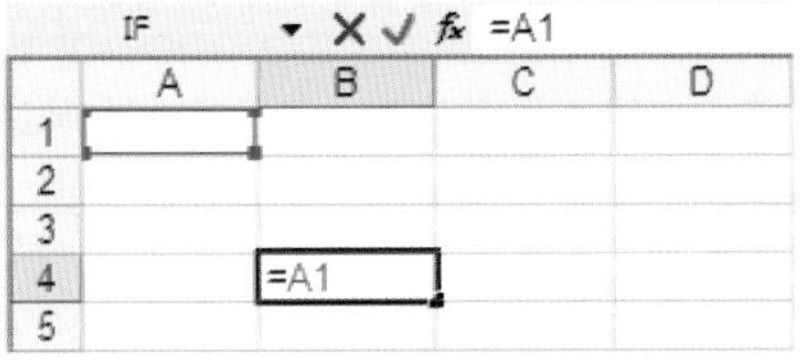

Figure 8.1

For example, if you copy cell **B4** to cell **C4**, the formula becomes **=B1**, because **B1** is the cell **3** above and one to the left of cell **C4**!

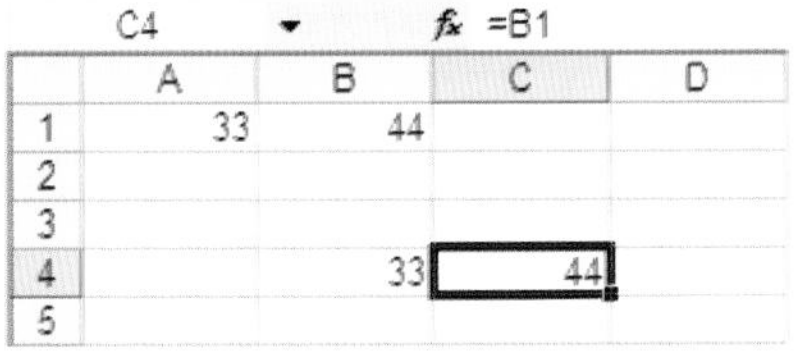

Figure 8.2

▶ Create a spreadsheet like the one above and have a play with copying and pasting cells and formulae.

▶ Close the spreadsheet when you have finished. There is no need to save it.

Absolute cell referencing

Absolute cell referencing is used when you always want to refer to the same cell. We'll work through the project below to demonstrate when to use absolute cell referencing.

Project: Car Imports

Open a new workbook. Copy the screenshot below, entering all the cell contents and copying the formatting.

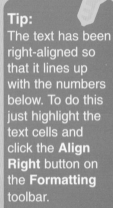

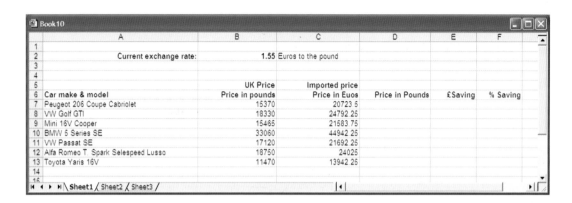

Figure 8.3

First we need to enter a formula to calculate the price of the imported cars in pounds. The price will be calculated using the current exchange rate which is entered at the top of the sheet.

Click in cell **D7**. Enter the formula **=C7/B2**. (To convert Euros to Pounds, you need to divide the Euro amount by the exchange rate). Press **Enter**.

We need the same formula in all the cells in that column, from **D7** to **D13**. Let's see what happens when we copy the formula down.

Click in cell **D7**. Click and drag the small handle on the bottom right of the cell down to cell **D13**.

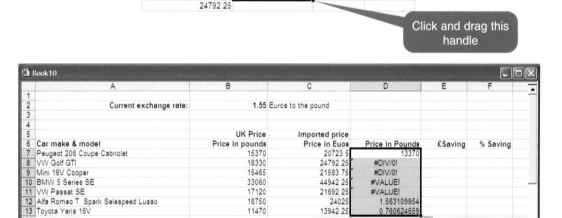

Figure 8.4

Excel has automatically used relative cell referencing, and as you can see, it hasn't worked!

 Click cell **D8** to see what formula is there.

The formula bar shows **=C8/B3**. What is in cell **B3**? Nothing! Take a look at the other formulae in the column. Can you see what has happened?

We should have used absolute cell referencing, as we always want the formula to refer to cell **B2** where the exchange rate is.

 Select cells **D8** to **D13** and press the **Delete** key.

 Click in cell **D7**. We need to alter the formula to make **B2** an absolute cell reference.

For absolute cell referencing, all you do is add a **$** symbol in front of the column AND row. You can put the symbol in front of the column only, but this will mean that when you copy the formula, only the column part of the formula will be kept constant. The same goes for rows.

 Change the formula in cell **D7** to **=C7/$B$2**.

	A	B	C	D	E	F
	1F ▾ X ✓ ƒx =C7/$B$2					
1						
2	Current exchange rate:	1.55	Euros to the pound			
3						
4						
5		UK Price	Imported price			
6	Car make & model	Price in pounds	Price in Euos	Price in Pounds	£Saving	% Saving
7	Peugeot 206 Coupe Cabriolet	15370	20723.5	=C7/$B$2		
8	VW Golf GTI	18330	24792.25			
9	Mini 16V Cooper	15465	21583.75			
10	BMW 5 Series SE	33060	44942.25			
11	VW Passat SE	17120	21692.25			
12	Alfa Romeo T. Spark Selespeed Lusso	18750	24025			
13	Toyota Yaris 16V	11470	13942.25			
14						

Figure 8.5

 Now copy the formula to the other cells in the column.

	A	B	C	D	E	F
	D7 ▾ ƒx =C7/$B$2					
1						
2	Current exchange rate:	1.55	Euros to the pound			
3						
4						
5		UK Price	Imported price			
6	Car make & model	Price in pounds	Price in Euos	Price in Pounds	£Saving	% Saving
7	Peugeot 206 Coupe Cabriolet	15370	20723.5	13370		
8	VW Golf GTI	18330	24792.25	15995		
9	Mini 16V Cooper	15465	21583.75	13925		
10	BMW 5 Series SE	33060	44942.25	28995		
11	VW Passat SE	17120	21692.25	13995		
12	Alfa Romeo T. Spark Selespeed Lusso	18750	24025	15500		
13	Toyota Yaris 16V	11470	13942.25	8995		
14						

Figure 8.6

That seems to have worked!

 Save the worksheet as **Cars** by clicking the **Save** icon.

Entering the other formulae

▶ You need to enter a formula for the **£Saving** column. For this, use the formula:

UK Price in Pounds – Imported Price in Pounds

▶ Copy the formula down the whole column. Do you need relative or absolute cell referencing for this?

Your spreadsheet should look like this – check your formulae if you're getting different figures.

E7	▾	fx =B7-D7			
	A	B	C	D	E	F

	A	B	C	D	E	F
1						
2	Current exchange rate:		1.55 Euros to the pound			
3						
4						
5		UK Price	Imported price			
6	Car make & model	Price in pounds	Price in Euos	Price in Pounds	£Saving	% Saving
7	Peugeot 206 Coupe Cabriolet	15370	20723.5	13370	2000	
8	VW Golf GTI	18330	24792.25	15995	2335	
9	Mini 16V Cooper	15465	21583.75	13925	1540	
10	BMW 5 Series SE	33060	44942.25	28995	4065	
11	VW Passat SE	17120	21692.25	13995	3125	
12	Alfa Romeo T. Spark Selespeed Lusso	18750	24025	15500	3250	
13	Toyota Yaris 16V	11470	13942.25	8995	2475	
14						

Figure 8.7

Calculating a percentage

We also need a formula for the **% Saving** column.

▶ Enter the formula for this calculation in cell **F7**:

£Saving / UK Price in Pounds

It might look like the answer is 0 – this is because there are no decimal places shown.

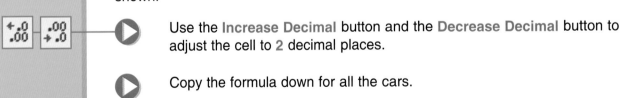

▶ Use the **Increase Decimal** button and the **Decrease Decimal** button to adjust the cell to **2** decimal places.

▶ Copy the formula down for all the cars.

▶ To turn them into percentages, select cells **F7** to **F13** then click the **Percent Style** on the **Formatting** toolbar.

	A	B	C	D	E	F
		F7		▼	_fx_ =E7/B7	
1						
2		Current exchange rate:	1.55	Euros to the pound		
3						
4						
5			UK Price	Imported price		
6	Car make & model		Price in pounds	Price in Euos	Price in Pounds	£Saving	% Saving
7	Peugeot 206 Coupe Cabriolet		15370	20723 5	13370	2000	13%
8	VW Golf GTI		18330	24792 25	15995	2335	13%
9	Mini 16V Cooper		15465	21583 75	13925	1540	10%
10	BMW 5 Series SE		33060	44942 25	28995	4065	12%
11	VW Passat SE		17120	21692 25	13995	3125	18%
12	Alfa Romeo T. Spark Selespeed Lusso		18750	24025	15500	3250	17%
13	Toyota Yaris 16V		11470	13942 25	8995	2475	22%
14						

Figure 8.8

▶ Have a play with the exchange rate. At what exchange rate does the **%
Saving** become zero for the **Mini**?

The currency format

Now we'll change the format of some of the columns to give them the **Currency**
number type.

▶ Select cells **B7** to **B13**, then hold down **Ctrl** while selecting cells **D7** to **E13**.

▶ Right-click anywhere within the selected cells to bring up the shortcut menu.

▶ Select **Format Cells** from the menu.

▶ Select **Currency** from the **Category** list (make sure the **Number** tab is
selected). Set the **Decimal places** to **0**. Excel should choose the £ symbol
by default, which is fine.

Tip:
Remember to
save your
workbook at
regular intervals.

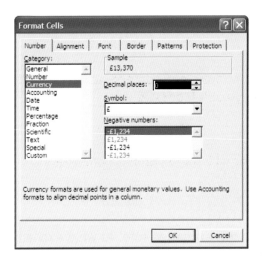

Figure 8.9

▶ Click **OK**.

▶ Repeat this for the **Euro** column. Remember to choose the **Euro** symbol from the **Symbol** list.

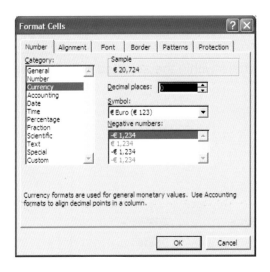

Figure 8.10

Your screen should now look like the one below.

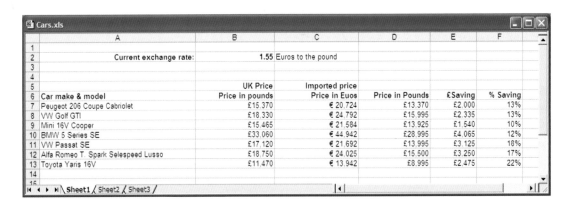

	A	B	C	D	E	F
1						
2	Current exchange rate:	1.55	Euros to the pound			
3						
4						
5		UK Price	Imported price			
6	Car make & model	Price in pounds	Price in Euos	Price in Pounds	£Saving	% Saving
7	Peugeot 206 Coupe Cabriolet	£15.370	€ 20,724	£13.370	£2.000	13%
8	VW Golf GTI	£18.330	€ 24,792	£15.995	£2.335	13%
9	Mini 16V Cooper	£15.465	€ 21,584	£13.925	£1.540	10%
10	BMW 5 Series SE	£33.060	€ 44.942	£28.995	£4.065	12%
11	VW Passat SE	£17.120	€ 21,692	£13.995	£3.125	18%
12	Alfa Romeo T. Spark Selespeed Lusso	£18.750	€ 24.025	£15.500	£3.250	17%
13	Toyota Yaris 16V	£11.470	€ 13.942	£8.995	£2.475	22%
14						

Sheet1 / Sheet2 / Sheet3 /

Figure 8.11

Merge and centre cell contents

You can easily merge and centre cell contents using the button on the **Formatting** toolbar. This is particularly useful for titles.

 Select cells **C5** and **D5**. Click the **Merge and Centre** button. ———————

That makes it a bit clearer which the imported prices are.

Adding a date field

We will add a date to show when the **Current exchange rate** was last updated.

 Add the fields as shown below in the screenshot.

	A	B	C	D	E	F
1						
2	Current exchange rate:	1.55	Euros to the pound	Updated:	14/03/2003	
3						
4						
5		UK Price	Imported price			
6	Car make & model	Price in pounds	Price in Euos	Price in Pounds	£Saving	% Saving
7	Peugeot 206 Coupe Cabriolet	£15.370	€ 20.724	£13.370	£2.000	13%
8	VW Golf GTI	£18.330	€ 24.792	£15.995	£2.335	13%
9	Mini 16V Cooper	£15.465	€ 21.584	£13.925	£1.540	10%
10	BMW 5 Series SE	£33.060	€ 44.942	£28.995	£4.065	12%
11	VW Passat SE	£17.120	€ 21.692	£13.995	£3.125	18%
12	Alfa Romeo T. Spark Selespeed Lusso	£18.750	€ 24.025	£15.500	£3.250	17%
13	Toyota Yaris 16V	£11.470	€ 13.942	£8.995	£2.475	22%
14						

Sheet1 / Sheet2 / Sheet3 /

Figure 8.12

 Now right-click in the date field, and select **Format Cells** from the shortcut menu that appears.

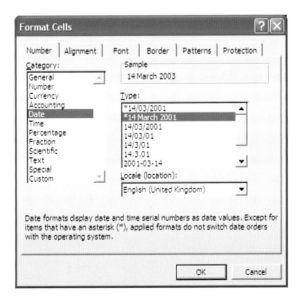

Figure 8.13

63

▶ Excel has already guessed that you want the **Date** category. Pick a date **Type** from the right-hand list. Note that although it looks like Excel has the day and month mixed up, it should get it right when you click **OK**.

▶ You might need to widen column **E** to display the whole date.

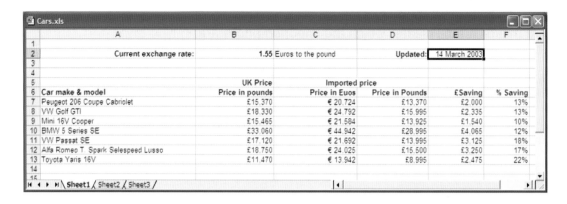

	A	B	C	D	E	F
1						
2	Current exchange rate:	1.55	Euros to the pound	Updated:	14 March 2003	
3						
4						
5		UK Price	Imported price			
6	Car make & model	Price in pounds	Price in Euos	Price in Pounds	£ Saving	% Saving
7	Peugeot 206 Coupe Cabriolet	£15.370	€ 20.724	£13.370	£2.000	13%
8	VW Golf GTI	£18.330	€ 24.792	£15.995	£2.335	13%
9	Mini 16V Cooper	£15.465	€ 21.584	£13.925	£1.540	10%
10	BMW 5 Series SE	£33.060	€ 44.942	£28.995	£4.065	12%
11	VW Passat SE	£17.120	€ 21.692	£13.995	£3.125	18%
12	Alfa Romeo T. Spark Selespeed Lusso	£18.750	€ 24.025	£15.500	£3.250	17%
13	Toyota Yaris 16V	£11.470	€ 13.942	£8.995	£2.475	22%
14						
15						

Figure 8.14

Wrapping cell content

Some of the car makes & models are quite long. It would look neater if the longer descriptions ran onto two lines, rather than making the column extra-wide to fit them.

▶ Select cell **A12**, then right-click it. Select **Format Cells** from the shortcut menu that appears.

▶ The **Format Cells** dialogue box appears. Click the **Alignment** tab.

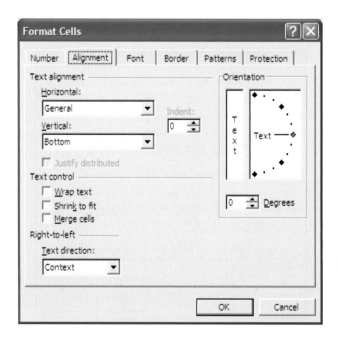

Figure 8.15

▶ Under the **Text Control** section, click the check box next to **Wrap text**. Click **OK**.

10	BMW 5 Series SE	£33,060
11	VW Passat SE	£17,120
12	Alfa Romeo T. Spark	£18,750
13	Toyota Yaris 16V	£11,470
14		
15		

▶ Now resize column **A** so that it is too small to fit all the words on one line.

▶ Widen row **12** by clicking and dragging between the row headers of row **12** and row **13**.

10	BMW 5 Series SE	£33,060
11	VW Passat SE	£17,120
12	Alfa Romeo T. Spark Selespeed Lusso	£18,750
13	Toyota Yaris 16V	£11,470
14		

The text just fills onto the next line!

▶ Repeat this for some of the other cells where the make & model description is long.

▶ Now make the column headings in row **6** wrap over two lines.

▶ We need to move the **Updated** field over to the right. Select cells **D2** and **E2**, then click and drag the border of the selection to the right.

	A	B	C	D	E	F	
1							
2	Current exchange rate:	1.55	Euros to the pound		Updated:	14 March 2003	
3							
4							
5		UK Price	Imported price				
6	Car make & model	Price in pounds	Price in Euos	Price in Pounds	£ Saving	% Saving	
7	Peugeot 206 Coupe Cabriolet	£15,370	€ 20,724	£13,370	£2,000	13%	
8	VW Golf GTI	£18,330	€ 24,792	£15,995	£2,335	13%	
9	Mini 16V Cooper	£15,465	€ 21,584	£13,925	£1,540	10%	
10	BMW 5 Series SE	£33,060	€ 44,942	£28,995	£4,065	12%	
11	VW Passat SE	£17,120	€ 21,692	£13,995	£3,125	18%	
12	Alfa Romeo T. Spark Selespeed Lusso	£18,750	€ 24,025	£15,500	£3,250	17%	
13	Toyota Yaris 16V	£11,470	€ 13,942	£8,995	£2,475	22%	
14							

Figure 8.16

Adding borders

We'll just quickly add some borders to make the headings a little clearer.

▶ Select cells **B5** and **B6**. Click the small down-arrow on the **Borders** icon on the **Formatting** toolbar.

▶ There are lots of different types of borders to choose from. Select the one shown.

Now select cells **C5** to **D6**. You don't need to click the down-arrow this time, just click the middle of the **Borders** icon. It will automatically create the same sort of border as before.

Repeat this for the various groups of cells, until your spreadsheet looks something like the one below.

	A	B	C	D	E	F	G
1							
2	Current exchange rate:	1.55	Euros to the pound		Updated:	14 March 2003	
3							
4							
5		UK Price	Imported price				
6	Car make & model	Price in pounds	Price in Euos	Price in Pounds	£Saving	% Saving	
7	Peugeot 206 Coupe Cabriolet	£15.370	€ 20.724	£13.370	£2.000	13%	
8	VW Golf GTI	£18.330	€ 24.792	£15.995	£2.335	13%	
9	Mini 16V Cooper	£15.465	€ 21.584	£13.925	£1.540	10%	
10	BMW 5 Series SE	£33.060	€ 44.942	£28.995	£4.065	12%	
11	VW Passat SE	£17.120	€ 21.692	£13.995	£3.125	18%	
12	Alfa Romeo T. Spark Selespeed Lusso	£18.750	€ 24.025	£15.500	£3.250	17%	
13	Toyota Yaris 16V	£11.470	€ 13.942	£8.995	£2.475	22%	
14							
15							

Figure 8.17

Finally, draw one big border around the table, using the slightly thicker border.

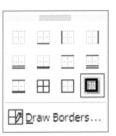

	A	B	C	D	E	F	G
1							
2	Current exchange rate:	1.55	Euros to the pound		Updated:	14 March 2003	
3							
4							
5		UK Price	Imported price				
6	Car make & model	Price in pounds	Price in Euos	Price in Pounds	£Saving	% Saving	
7	Peugeot 206 Coupe Cabriolet	£15.370	€ 20.724	£13.370	£2.000	13%	
8	VW Golf GTI	£18.330	€ 24.792	£15.995	£2.335	13%	
9	Mini 16V Cooper	£15.465	€ 21.584	£13.925	£1.540	10%	
10	BMW 5 Series SE	£33.060	€ 44.942	£28.995	£4.065	12%	
11	VW Passat SE	£17.120	€ 21.692	£13.995	£3.125	18%	
12	Alfa Romeo T. Spark Selespeed Lusso	£18.750	€ 24.025	£15.500	£3.250	17%	
13	Toyota Yaris 16V	£11.470	€ 13.942	£8.995	£2.475	22%	
14							
15							

Figure 8.18

Click **Print Preview** to see what your spreadsheet will look like when printed. You'll need to change the **Page Orientation** to fit it all on one page.

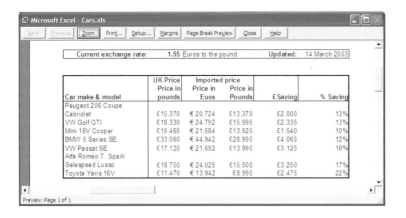

Figure 8.19

▶ Click **Close** to exit **Print Preview**.

Find and replace

There aren't many records in this spreadsheet, but in larger spreadsheets it is useful to be able to search for a particular value.

Finding a cell containing a particular word or value

▶ Select **Edit**, **Find** from the menu.

▶ Enter **VW** in the **Find what:** box.

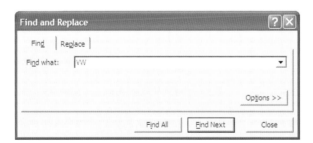

Figure 8.20

▶ Click **Find Next**.

▶ Excel makes the cell containing **VW** the active cell. Click **Find Next** again.

Excel moves to the second cell containing **VW**.

Replacing a word or value

If you have spelt a name wrongly in several different places in a spreadsheet, it is useful to set Excel to find and replace each instance of the word. For practice, we'll replace the word **VW** with **Volkswagen**.

▶ Click the **Replace** tab at the top of the **Search and Replace** dialogue box.

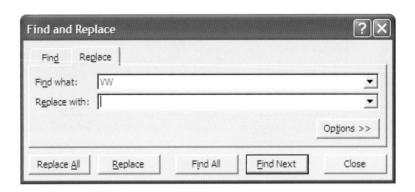

Figure 8.21

▶ Type **Volkswagen** in the **Replace with:** box.

▶ Click the **Replace All** button.

Figure 8.22

▶ Click **OK**. Notice that **VW** has now become **Volkswagen**. Click **Close**.

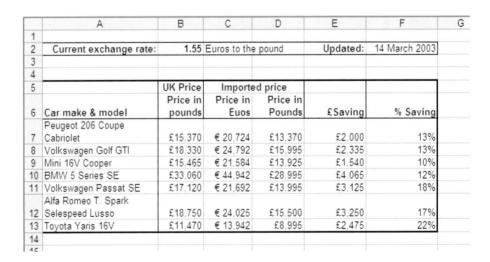

Figure 8.23

Adding Headers and Footers

Headers and footers are useful for automatically inserting information such as the current date and page numbers on larger documents.

 Select **View**, **Header and Footer** from the menu.

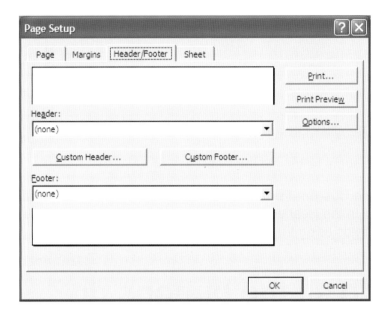

Figure 8.24

 Click the **Custom Header** button.

 Click in the **Center Section** box and type **Car Import Savings Sheet**.

This title text should be bold, we'll do this now.

 Highlight the text you have just written, then click the **Font** button. ————

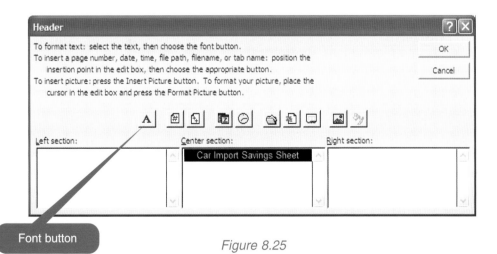

Font button

Figure 8.25

 Make the text **12** point and bold.

Tip:
You can also view the Header and Footer in the **Page Setup** dialogue box. Click **File, Page Setup** then click the **Header** and **Footer** tab.

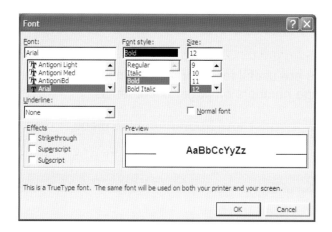

Figure 8.26

▶ Click **OK**. Click **OK** again to exit the **Header** dialogue box.

Now we'll insert some fields into the **Footer**.

▶ Click the **Custom Footer** button. You can enter text here just the same as you did in the Header. This time though we won't enter any text, we'll just insert fields using the buttons provided.

What do all the buttons do?

There are quite a few buttons to choose from!

▶ To find out what a button is called, and what it does, right-click on a button then click **What's This?**

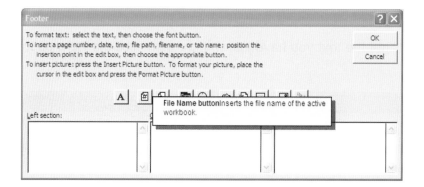

Figure 8.27

A small box pops up telling you what the button does.

Inserting the file name

▶ Click somewhere in the **Left section** box.

 ▶ Click the **Filename** button.

Inserting the worksheet name

▶ Type a comma and a space after the **Filename** expression then click the **Worksheet Name** button.

Inserting the page number

This is only really useful in longer documents, but we'll add it anyway for practice.

▶ Click in the **Center Section**. Click the **Page Number** button.

Inserting the date

▶ Click in the **Right Section**, then click the **Date** button.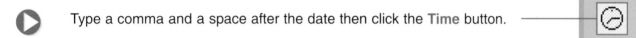

Inserting the time

▶ Type a comma and a space after the date then click the **Time** button.

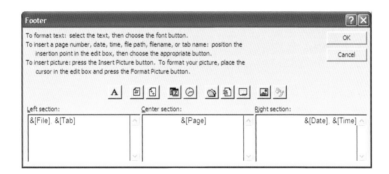

Figure 8.28

▶ Click **OK**.

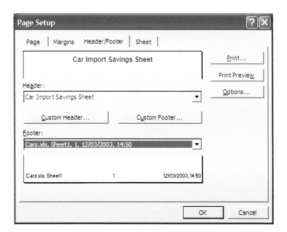

Figure 8.29

You can see what the headers and footers will look like in the **Page Setup** window. Click **OK** when you're happy with how it looks.

Click **Print Preview** to see what the sheet will look like when printed.

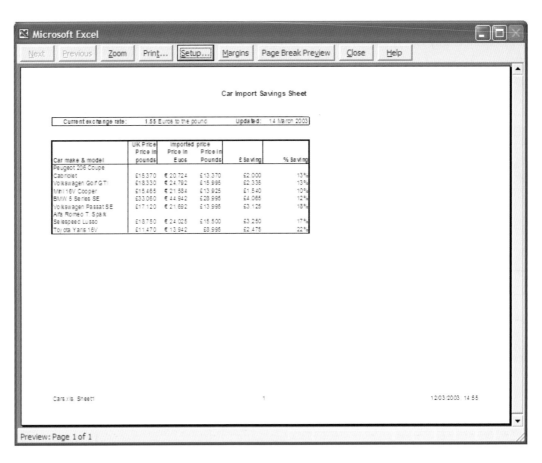

Figure 8.30

Print the spreadsheet if you like, otherwise click the **Close** button.

Save and close the spreadsheet.

Chapter 9
If... Then... Else...

In this chapter we'll create a spreadsheet for a Mirror shop. The shop offers cut-to-size mirrors, and they need a spreadsheet that will give an instant quote for a customer, given the required size.

Project: Create a spreadsheet to produce instant quotes

The shop offers only one thickness of glass, 6mm. It offers a choice of polished, or polished and bevelled edges.

The price of the mirror is dependent on the surface area and the perimeter length.

These are the prices:

£32 per square metre of surface area

£1.70 per linear metre of perimeter for polished edges

£2.10 per linear metre of perimeter for polished and bevelled edges

 Open a new workbook, type in the text, format the text and add the borders so that your spreadsheet looks like the one below.

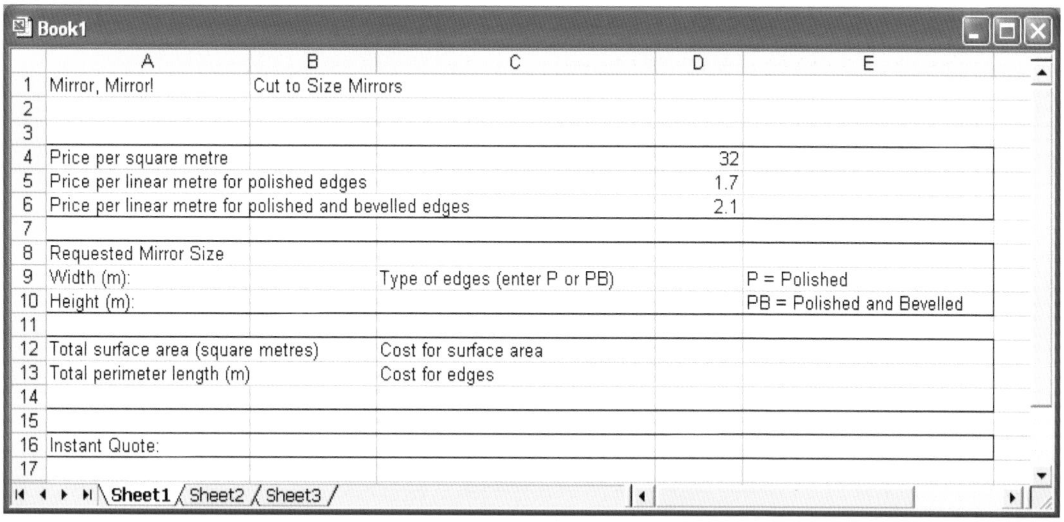

	A	B	C	D	E
1	Mirror, Mirror!	Cut to Size Mirrors			
2					
3					
4	Price per square metre			32	
5	Price per linear metre for polished edges			1.7	
6	Price per linear metre for polished and bevelled edges			2.1	
7					
8	Requested Mirror Size				
9	Width (m):		Type of edges (enter P or PB)		P = Polished
10	Height (m):				PB = Polished and Bevelled
11					
12	Total surface area (square metres)		Cost for surface area		
13	Total perimeter length (m)		Cost for edges		
14					
15					
16	Instant Quote:				
17					

Book1

Sheet1 / Sheet2 / Sheet3 /

Figure 9.1

Changing font style and size

We need to give the title and some of the other headings a bit of a makeover.

▶ Select cell **A1**. On the **Formatting** toolbar, select size **26** font.

▶ Now change the font. Choose any font you like the look of. Make it bold also by clicking the **Bold** icon.

▶ You need to move the contents of cell **B1** to cell **D1**. Make sure cell **B1** is selected, then click and drag the black border over to cell **D1**.

▶ Change some more of the headings and formats to look like the screenshot below.

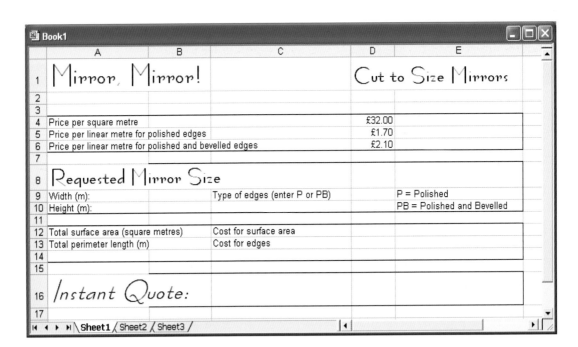

Figure 9.2

Adding the formulae

We'll do some more formatting in a minute. First we have to enter the formulae.

▶ The calculation for **Total surface area** is **Width** x **Height** . Enter the formula in cell **B12** as **=B9*B10**.

▶ The calculation for **Total perimeter length** is **2 x (Width + Height)**. Enter the formula as **=2*(B9+B10)**. You will need the brackets in the formula.

▶ Enter the formula for **Cost for surface area**. It should be **=B12*D4**.

▶ Save the workbook as **Mirrors**. —————————————————————

Enter some data

▶ Try out your formulae by entering the length and width of a mirror.

▶ Enter either **P** or **PB** where specified.

IF statements

Our calculation for the **Cost for edges** has to include an **IF** statement, so it can calculate the cost for either **polished** or **polished and bevelled** edges.

IF edges are **polished** THEN Cost for edges = perimeter length***D5**

IF edges are **bevelled** THEN Cost for edges = perimeter length ***D6**

Breaking these statements down further:

IF cell D9 = **P** THEN cell D13 = B13***D5**

IF cell D9 = **PB** THEN cell D13 = B13***D6**

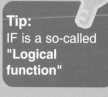

Tip:
IF is a so-called **"Logical function"**

▶ Select cell **D13**. Click the **Paste Function** button to the left of the Formula bar.

D13 ▼ *fx*

Paste function button

▶ Select **IF** from the **Select a function** list. If you cannot see it in the list, change the category **Logical**.

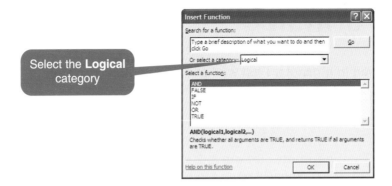

Select the **Logical** category

Figure 9.3

▶ Click **OK**.

▶ Enter the following formulae into the **Function Arguments** dialogue box.

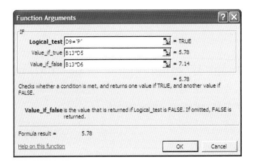

Figure 9.4

▶ Click **OK**.

▶ Format all the currency cells to show pound signs, and have **2** decimal places if you haven't done so already.

▶ Finally fill in the last formula for the total cost, next to the Instant **Quote** heading. It should be **=SUM(D12:D13)**.

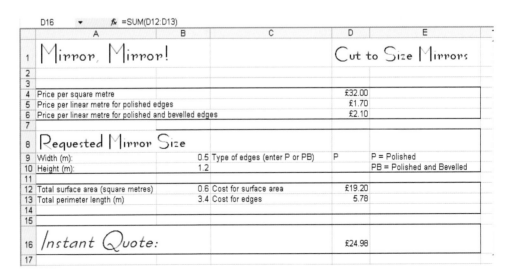

Figure 9.5

76

Adding some colour

It would be nice if the spreadsheet was a bit more colourful. We can do this by changing the font colour and the background fill colour.

Changing the font colour

▶ Select cell **A1**.

▶ Click the down arrow on the **Font Colour** button. —————————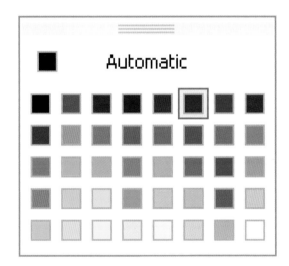

▶ Click any colour to select it.

Changing the background fill colour

▶ With cell **A1** still selected, click the down arrow on the **Background Fill** button.

▶ Click to select a colour.

Aligning cell content

You can set where the text appears in a cell – left, right, top, bottom or centre.

▶ Widen **Row 1** by clicking and dragging between the row selectors of **Row 1** and **Row 2**.

▶ Select cells **A1** and **D1**. Right-click somewhere in a selected cell.

▶ Select **Format Cells** from the menu.

▶ Click the **Alignment** tab. Select **Centre** in the **Vertical Alignment** box. Take a look at the other alignment options – they might come in useful!

Tip:
You use the **Format Cells** dialogue box to change the alignment of the cells. You can make the text vertical if you like!

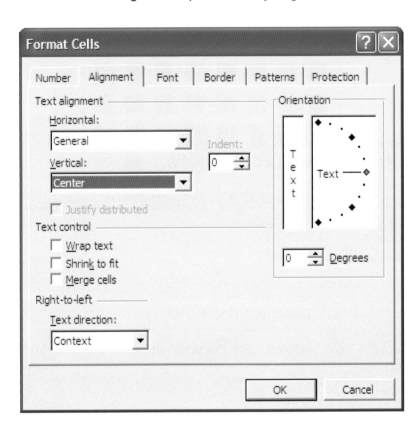

Figure 9.6

Cell orientation

You can change the orientation of the text in the cells using the Format Cells dialogue box.

 Click and drag the red dot so that the text is slightly diagonal.

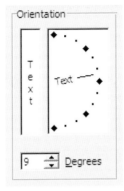

 Click **OK**.

Add some more colours, and play around with the formatting so that your spreadsheet looks something like the one below.

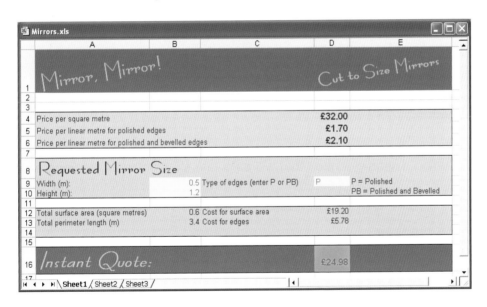

Figure 9.7

 Enter some different values for the width and height of the mirror. You can also change the prices.

 Save and close the spreadsheet when you're happy with it.

Chapter 10
VLookup

In this chapter we will create a spreadsheet that could be used by staff in ski rental shops. It will allow the staff to type in the customer's weight and ski level ability, and will then display the optimum ski length for them.

Project: Create a spreadsheet for a ski rental shop

Planning the spreadsheet

The first step is to find out what the ideal ski sizes are for skiers of various weights and abilities – any rental shop will probably have paper tables which they use to look up ski sizes. The aim of this spreadsheet is to computerise this paper chart to eliminate the need for staff to manually look up ski sizes.

The next step is to plan how the application will work. It must be quick and easy to use, so some thought needs to go into how the information is laid out and presented.

We will develop a simple version that will calculate ski lengths for beginners and intermediates only, and for one type of ski. If you like, you can later develop the spreadsheet to include more options.

Building the spreadsheet

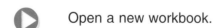 Open a new workbook.

First we'll enter the recommended ski lengths for beginners.

▶ Type the heading **Ski Length Calculator** in cell **A1**.

 ▶ Centre the heading across cells **A1** to **D1** using the **Merge and Center** button. Have a play with the font size and style, and colour the cell to make the heading look a bit more interesting.

▶ Enter the rest of the data shown in Figure 10.1.

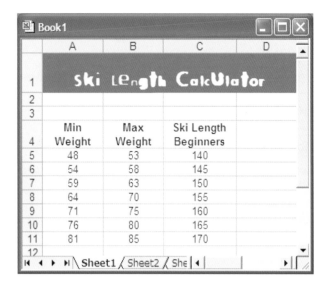

Figure 10.1

Tip:
You'll need to use the **Wrap text** function to get the titles to run onto two lines like this. To do this, right click on the relevant cells and select **Format Cells** from the shortcut menu. Click the **Alignment** tab then the **Wrap text** check box.

Naming Ranges

It is possible to rename individual cells and also cell ranges. Here we will name a cell range to make referring to the range much easier. By referring to named cells you will automatically be using absolute referencing.

▶ Highlight cells **A5** to **C11**.

▶ Select **Insert**, **Name**, **Define** from the main menu.

▶ Name the selected range **SkiLength**.

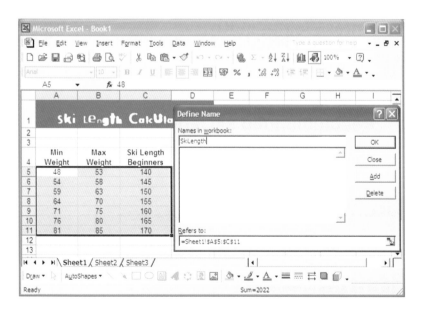

Figure 10.2: Naming a range of cells

▶ Click **OK**.

81

Moving and renaming sheets

We need a main screen into which the customer's weight will need to be entered.

▶ Drag the sheet tab for **Sheet2** to the left of **Sheet1**.

▶ Right-click the **Sheet2** tab and rename it **MainScreen**.

▶ Rename **Sheet1 SkiLengthChart**.

▶ Delete **Sheet3**.

Designing the user screen

Now we can display the screen that the ski shop staff will enter the data into, and which will display the correct length of ski for the customer.

▶ Click on the **MainScreen** sheet tab.

▶ Copy the design as shown in Figure 10.3.

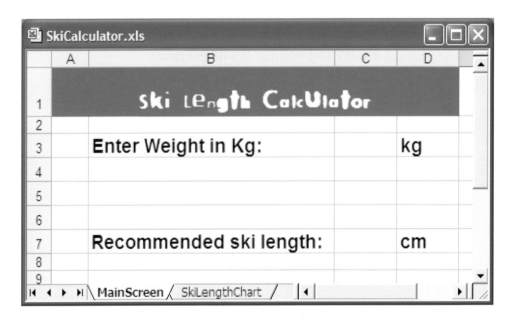

Figure 10.3: The front screen

▶ Save your work as **SkiCalculator**.

Adding validation to cells

Validation is the checking of input data by software, to make sure that it is sensible or reasonable.

In this case, validation is used to make sure that when the customer weight is entered, it is within the allowed range. This reduces the chances of the user making an error when entering the weight.

▶ Click in cell **C3** on the **MainScreen** sheet.

▶ Select **Data**, **Validation** from the menu.

▶ Select **Whole number** from the first drop-down list. You are then asked for a data range. Enter **48** as the minimum weight and **85** as the maximum.

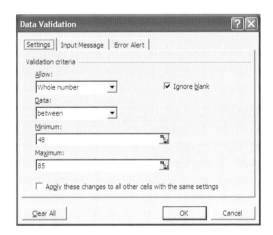

Figure 10.4: Adding validation to a cell

▶ Now we need to enter an **Input Message**. Click the **Input Message** tab and enter the text as shown in the screenshot below.

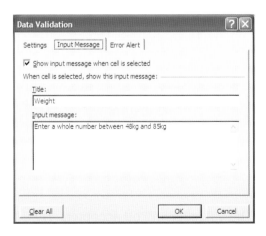

Figure 10.5: Entering an Input Message

Finally, we'll enter an **Error Alert** message. Select the **Error Alert** tab at the top of the dialogue box.

The message we enter here is the message that will appear if someone enters an invalid value.

 Choose a **Style** from the left drop-down list. Type the message **Weight must be a whole number between 48kg and 85kg**. Give it the title **Weight**.

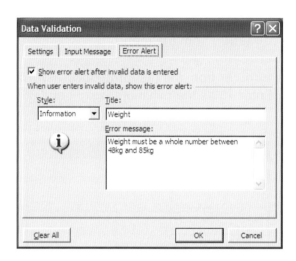

Figure 10.6: Adding an Error Alert

 Click **OK** to close the dialogue box.

Testing your validation

It is important to try and enter some invalid values into the cell to make sure that the validation rule works. You must make sure that it rejects invalid values but it is equally important to make sure that it accepts valid values – if not you'll have to go back and check the settings!

 Click in cell **C3**. You will see your **Input Message**. Try entering **45**. Press **Enter**.

Figure 10.7: Error!

 Now enter **59**. The value should be accepted. Try a few more values to convince yourself the validation rule is working correctly.

 Save your work.

The VLookup function

The **VLookup** function is what we'll use to automatically display the correct ski length based on the weight entered.

▶ Select cell **C7**. Click the down-arrow next to the **AutoSum** button. Select ———— [Σ ▼]
  More Functions....

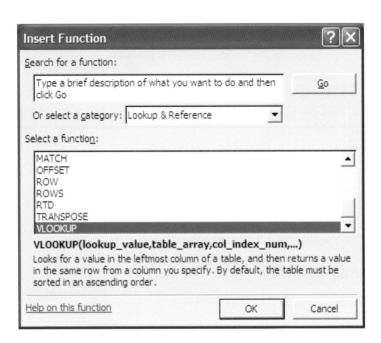

Figure 10.8: The VLookup function

▶ Find **VLookup** at the bottom of the function list. Click **OK**.

▶ The **Lookup_value** is the cell you want to find in a table. You need to enter **C3** here.

▶ Enter **SkiLength** in the **Table_array** box. This is the range that contains all of the lengths on the **SkiLengthChart** sheet.

VLookup will look for the value you entered in cell **C3** in the left-most column of the range that you entered – that is the **Minimum Weight** column. If it can't find the exact value (for example, if you enter **65**) it will default to the nearest value less than **65** and find the ski length for someone whose minimum weight is **64**. For this reason Vlookup will not work unless the **Table_array** you refer to is sorted in **Ascending** order.

▶ Now you need to find the ski length from the third column in the table, so enter **3** in the **Col_index_num** box.

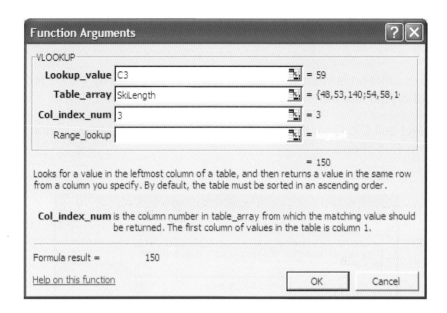

Figure 10.9: Using VLookup to find a ski length

▶ Click **OK**.

▶ Try changing the customer weight in cell **C3**. What happens?

▶ Save the spreadsheet.

Chapter 11
Macros and Buttons

In this chapter we'll add a new column to the ski length chart to include recommended ski lengths for intermediate level skiers. We'll then use macros and buttons on the main screen so that the user can specify whether the customer is a beginner or intermediate.

▶ Load Excel and open the **SkiCalculator** spreadsheet.

▶ Click on the **SkiLengthChart** sheet tab. Add a column of recommended ski lengths for intermediate level skiers as shown below.

SkiCalculator.xls				
	A	B	C	D	E

	Ski Length Calculator				

	Min Weight	Max Weight	Ski Length Beginners	Ski Length Intermediate
5	48	53	140	150
6	54	58	145	155
7	59	63	150	160
8	64	70	155	165
9	71	75	160	170
10	76	80	165	175
11	81	85	170	175

⧏ ◀ ▶ ⧐ \ MainScreen \ **SkiLengthChart** / ◀ | ▶

Figure 11.1

Redefining a named range

▶ Now that we've added another column, we need to redefine the **SkiLength** range that we named in the last chapter.

▶ Select **Insert**, **Name**, **Define** from the menu.

▶ Select **SkiLength**. In the **Refers to:** box, click the **Collapse Dialogue** button and select cells **A5** to **D11**.

▶ Press **Enter**. Click **OK**.

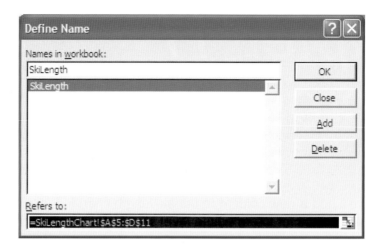

Figure 11.2: Redefining a named range

The Format Painter button

▶ Return to the **MainScreen** sheet.

▶ In cell **B5** type **Enter Skier Ability Level:**.

▶ Select cell **B3** and click the **Format Painter button**.

▶ Now click in cell **B5**.

Figure 11.3: Using Format Painter

The formatting of cell B3 will be copied to cell B5!

Selecting values from a drop-down list

In cell C5 the user needs to specify either Beginner or Intermediate. It would be nice if the user could select an option from a list rather than typing it in. This will be quicker and will eliminate the chances of the user making a spelling error; the computer wouldn't be able to recognise a mis-spelt word and would return either an error message or a wrong value.

 Click in cell **F2** and type **Beginner**. Type **Intermediate** in cell **F3**.

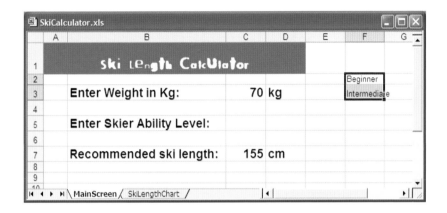

Figure 11.4

 Now click in cell **C5**. Select **Data**, **Validation...** from the menu.

 Under the **Settings** tab, choose **List** from the **Allow:** menu.

 Tab to the **Source:** box and on the spreadsheet, highlight cells **F2** to **F3**. Click **OK**.

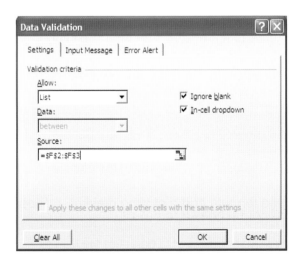

Figure 11.5: Validation

▶ Click on the small down-arrow next to cell **C5** and see what appears!

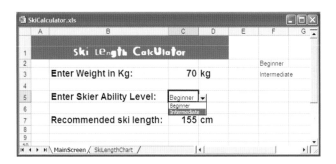

Figure 11.6

▶ You can colour the text in cells **F2** and **F3** white to hide it if you like.

If.. Then.. Else.. & VLookup

Now we need to add an **IF** statement to cell **C7** so that Excel looks up different ski lengths for beginners and intermediates; at the moment it is set up to give the ski lengths for beginners only.

The logic goes something like this:

If... Beginner is selected, **Then...** look up the ski length from the Beginner column, **Else...** look up the ski length from the Intermediate column.

To do the looking up, we will need to use the **VLookup** function again, so in fact we are using one function inside another. To start off with we will just do the **If... Then** part. When that works we can add the **Else...** part!

▶ Select cell **C7**. The formula needs to be amended like the example above.

▶ Click in the **Formula Bar** to edit the formula

▶ Position the cursor just after the = at the beginning of the formula.

▶ Type **IF(C5="Beginner",** but **DO NOT** press **Enter** yet!

VLOOKUP ▾ ✗ ✓ *fx* =If(C5="Beginner",VLOOKUP(C3,SkiLength,3)

Figure 11.7: Amending the formula

▶ At the end of the formula add a closing bracket). Press **Enter**.

C7 ▾ *fx* =IF(C5="Beginner",VLOOKUP(C3,SkiLength,3))

Figure 11.8: The If... Then... part of the new formula

▶ Test the new formula by choosing **Beginner** as the ability level and changing the customer's weight.

It should work! Now you can add the last part of the formula to tell Excel what to do if Intermediate is selected as the ability level.

▶ Click in cell **C7** and delete the last closing bracket). Type in a **comma** instead.

Now add another VLOOKUP formula to find the ski length for Intermediate skiers.

▶ Type in **VLOOKUP(C3, SkiLength,** but **DO NOT** press **Enter**!

This time you will need to look in the fourth column of the **SkiLength** table, so the last part of the **VLOOKUP** formula will be a **4** instead of a **3**.

▶ Enter a **4** and two closing brackets **))**. One for the **VLOOKUP** and one for the **IF** statement.

| VLOOKUP | ▾ ✕ ✓ ƒ× =IF(C5="Beginner",VLOOKUP(C3,SkiLength,3),VLOOKUP(C3,SkiLength,4)) |

Figure 11.9: Completing the If statement

▶ Make sure you've entered the formula correctly, then press **Enter**.

Test your new system!

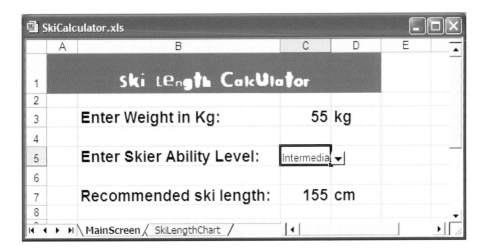

Figure 11.10

▶ Save your work.

Creating a menu screen

We need to create another new sheet which will display a brief menu of options. A menu screen would be more important if you had included a more comprehensive table of winter sports information, such as a table of snowboard sizes. As it is, the menu screen will give the user a choice of calculating the ski length or viewing the ski length chart.

▶ Right-click the sheet tab for **MainScreen** and insert a new worksheet.

▶ Right-click the new tab and select **Rename**. Type in **Menu** and press **Enter**.

▶ Right-click the tab again and select **Tab Colour...**

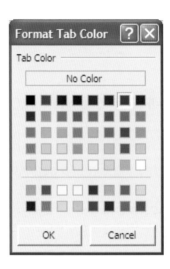

Figure 11.11: Changing the tab colour

▶ Change the colour to **Blue**. Click **OK**.

▶ Design a menu screen like the one below.

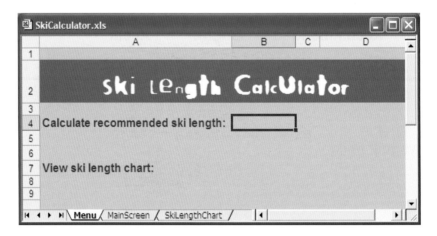

Figure 11.12: The menu screen

Adding clip art

▶ Select **Insert**, **Picture**, **Clip Art** from the menu.

▶ Select a suitable picture and move it into position on your menu screen.

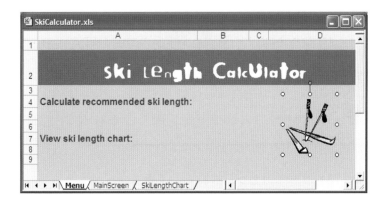

Figure 11.13: Adding clip art

▶ Save your work.

Macros

A macro is a series of commands that are stored and grouped to run as a single command when you activate it by using a particular keystroke combination or by pressing a button.

For this project, a simple macro will be used to go to the **MainScreen** sheet from the **Menu** sheet and put the cursor in cell **C3** ready to enter the customer's weight.

▶ Select the **Menu** worksheet.

▶ Select **Tools**, **Macro**, **Record New Macro...** from the menu.

▶ Call the macro **MainScreen**. Click **OK**.

Figure 11.14: Recording a macro

You will see the **Recording Toolbar** appear. You are now in recording mode. Everything you do now will be recorded by Excel. Be careful here!

▶ Click on the **MainScreen** tab.

▶ Click in cell **C3**.

▶ Click the **Stop Recording** button. All done!

Figure 11.15

Buttons

Now you need to add a button which will run the macro.

▶ Select the **Menu** sheet tab.

▶ Click **View**, **Toolbars**, **Forms** from the menu.

▶ Select the **Button** tool.

Figure 11.16

▶ Drag a small button onto your **Menu** screen, roughly over cells **B4** to **B5**.

▶ The **Assign Macro** box will appear. Select the **MainScreen** macro and click **OK**.

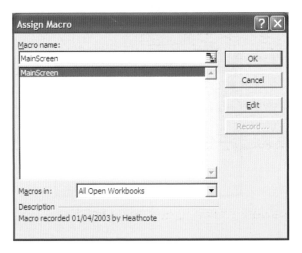

Figure 11.17: Assigning a macro to an object

94

If the button has handles round it then you can click on the text to edit it. If there are no handles, right-click the button and click **Edit Text**. Change the text on the button to say **Ski Calculator**.

When the handles are showing (to display handles, right-click the button, then left-click the button to close the shortcut menu) click and drag the handles so all the text is visible.

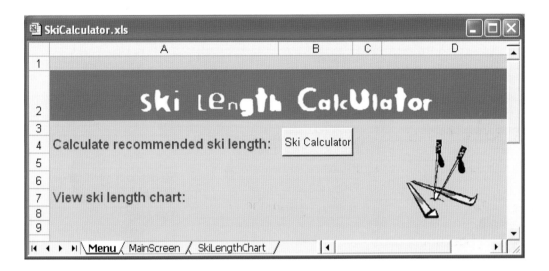

Figure 11.18

Test the new button!

Now use the same method to create a second button below the first. The second button should open the **SkiLengthChart** sheet.

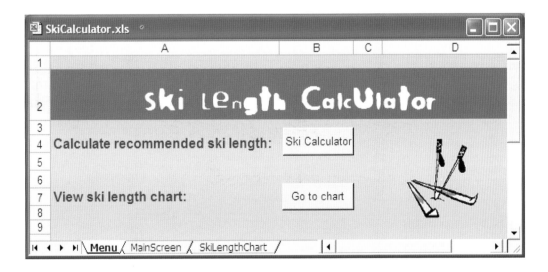

Figure 11.19

That's it! Save your work and go book a holiday!

Index